DISCARD

Can Black Mothers Raise Our Sons?

by Lawson Bush V

Front cover illustration by Tony Quaid
Copyright © 1999 by Lawson Bush V
First Edition, First Printing

Printed in the United States of America

ISBN: 0-913543-64-0

CONTENTS

ACKNOWLEDGMENTS

Because of the sacrifices of my parents, Catherine and Lawson Bush, IV, and the support of my best friends and siblings, Edward Bush, Regina Bush-Dean, and Rev. LaQuetta Bush-Simmons, my life achievements were made possible.

Additionally, I am thankful to my Dissertation Committee Members, Sheila Walker, Stanley Gaines, Lourdes Arguelles, and my advisor, friend, and Chair, Daryl Smith.

The Creator has sent me several mentors, Garret Duncan, Baba Cloyed Miller, Uncle Melvin, Donald Cheek, Willie Coleman, and Carl Wallace. The resources of the Office of Black Student Affairs have helped sustain me through my graduate studies. The Office of Teacher Education also deserves recognition for creating professional, intellectual, and personal space for me to grow.

I want to thank the children and staff of the Imani Saturday Academy; members of Antioch Missionary Baptist Church; and family members, including Nia, Khari, Jenise, Kirk, Kelvin, Triquetta, Aunt Gladys, Aunt Lena, Aunt Irma, Mama Cecil, Bessie Will, and all my folks in Mississippi.

My wife Tonia makes me believe I can conquer the world, and my daughter Chioma Agyei gives me the reason to conquer it.

To God be the glory.

OVERVIEW

Can mothers teach their sons how to become men? In recent years that question has been discussed and debated on Black radio, in Black magazines, workshops and conferences, and Black households across this nation. Yet, there is little research to inform those who participate in this argumentative discourse. Toward this end, this book examines how Black mothers participate in raising their sons to become Black men. An analysis of the historical, sociological, and biological variables that influence the construct of Black male sex roles is provided. Every parent, guardian, teacher, counselor, social worker, coach, spiritual leader, and psychologist must understand the dynamics and potential impact of these variables so that we may effectively raise Black males in the twenty-first century.

To help us gain a deeper insight into the Black mother-son relationship, 27 mothers, with at least one son, were selected from churches, a homeless shelter, schools, and other locations.[1] Twenty-three of the mothers, whose sons were ages 6–19, 24, and older, participated in face-to-face tape-recorded interviews. I interviewed at least one half of the participants' sons face-to-face. The remaining four mothers, whose sons were infants, participated in a group interview. I included both middle-class and lower-class participants in this study to shed some much needed light on Black families in both income groups.

As Joyce King and Carolyn Mitchell (1990) point out in their work, not only is there little information concerning Black mother and son relationships, but in all mother and son relationships, irrespective of race, ethnicity, or class. This anemia in the literature underscores the justification, significance, and need for this book and provides a unique opportunity to make groundbreaking contributions to the growing field of psychology, especially as it pertains to the study of the developmental process in males. The following chapters examine the developmental, sociological, biological, and historical factors concerning the construction of Black manhood and masculinity and how Black mothers raise their male children to adulthood. In Chapter 1, we begin to examine many of the complicated issues and dynamics surrounding this discussion. Manhood and masculinity are defined. In addition, a list of statistics is presented that illustrates the condition of Black males in this society.

Chapter 2 is a literature review of the research that seeks to explain the developmental process of Black males. I specifically address the sociohistorical dynamics of Black manhood and masculinity. In this chapter I ask the question, have Black males in the United States acquired their manhood? In the second section I address the many social factors involved in Black male development. The analysis explores the role Black women play in the development of boys to manhood, thus laying the foundation for effective parenting strategies. With the publication of *Can Black Mothers Raise Their Sons?* My hope is that this most important issue, which has been left out of the academic discussion, will finally receive the attention that is crucial to the survival of African American males.

Chapter 3 reviews the literature concerning Black mothers. We review some of the myths and stereotypes often used to unjustly characterize Black women. I present some of the demographics concerning Black single mothers.

This section explores popular assumptions made about the outcomes of single-mother families, with a special emphasis on how this family structure affects the lives of Black male children. Finally, I critique two studies that address mother-son relationships.

It is important that the reader gain an understanding of the developmental and sociohistorical influences discussed in Chapters 2 and 3 before entertaining the issue of Black mothers raising boys. Far too many individuals engage in this dialogue merely from a personal, non-historical, and emotional perspective. Thus, Chapters 2 and 3 provide the reader with the depth and context in which all conversations concerning this subject matter must be based. These two chapters lay the foundation for the entire book. However, if as a single Black mother you are doubting your ability to raise your son to manhood, I strongly recommend that you skip Chapters 2 and 3 and go directly to Chapters 4 and 5.

How Black mothers are raising their sons in the real world is the subject of Chapter 4 and the centerpiece of my research. Chapter 4 contains the information gleaned from my interviews and focus groups with mothers and sons. In the first section, we review the attributes Black mothers say they possess that help them raise their sons. The second section is an analysis of the participants' attitudes and beliefs about issues relating to Black males in the United States. In the third section, I construct a definition of manhood and masculinity drafted from the mothers' responses. In the final section, I present the methods Black mothers use to teach their sons life's lessons.

Chapter 5 is an analysis of the findings that were presented in Chapter 4. We examine an apparent paradox between what mothers do and what they believe in respect to raising their sons. We also examine research that attempts to correlate certain behavioral patterns to demographic data. Finally, we look at some potential threats to the effectiveness of Black motherhood.

In the first section of Chapter 6, we summarize the current research. In the last section, I conclude with my personal thoughts concerning this work, as well as advice from both mothers and sons on how to raise Black males.

Chapter 1
Introduction, Issues, and Statistics

The bottom line is this: if we are to develop as a people, enlightened education requires that gender distinctions be minimized to those areas where such distinctions are vital and necessary. Understand that I am not pushing for a gender-free society but a society where one is not oppressed due to sex, race, religion, etc.

It is obvious that women cannot be replaced as mothers, nor men as fathers without serious and often detrimental disruptions to the family.

Haki R. Madhubuti
Black Men: Obsolete, Single, Dangerous

While I was gathering information for this book, I went on a camping trip with young Black males, four to twelve years of age. Two of the young boys, with whom I have had prior experience, were very "whiney" and did not get along very well with the other boys. One of the boys was five years old; I have seen him often clinging to his mother's leg, not wanting to let her out of his sight. Both mothers are single parents. While on the camping trip, a group of men were standing together and we all seemed to be thinking the same thought: "These boys need a daddy." I slowly nodded my head in agreement. Already

1

I had begun to think about the implications of that statement in light of my research project.

I must admit that whiney boys irritate me, but not just because they are male. This is unacceptable behavior for boys and girls. Yet these questions remain: What made these young males act in this manner? Did their behavior have anything to do with the fact that they were being raised by women?

Shortly after the camping trip I had a conversation about this topic with a middle-aged Black woman I met while doing research in the library. She seemed very interested, although she did not have a son; she is a single mother of a ten-year-old girl. She told me that while she was in labor, she was terrified about the possibility of having a boy and not being able to raise him properly. As an educator, I have at least a dozen similar conversations every day. Inevitably, the conclusions are always the same: "Black boys need their fathers to be successful and to be men."

Black males have been labeled an "endangered species." The number of Black children under 18 years old living with one parent, mostly female, increased from 21.9 percent in 1960 to more than 50 percent in 1990 (U.S. Bureau of the Census, 1991) (see Table 1). Horrendous and frightening social circumstances face Black males every day. At the very least, we need to understand all the dynamics that involve Black males, including the interactions, both positive and negative, between Black single mothers and their sons. The quotations not only implicate

Black single mothers as having a negative effect on Black males, but they suggest that overexposure to women in general will have negative consequences.

Table 1

Percentage of Children under Age 18 Living with One Parent, by Race/Ethnicity for 1960, 1970, 1980, and 1990.

Race/Ethnicity	Year of Census Data			
	1960	1970	1980	1990
Black	21.9	31.8	45.8	54.8
White	7.1	8.7	15.1	19.2
Latino	N/A	N/A	21.1	30.0

(U.S. Bureau of the Census, 1991, p. 5)

On the other hand, while we engage and struggle with the issues germane to this research, we do not want to fall into the trap of blaming Black mothers for problems facing African Americans, nor do we want to say that Black fathers are obsolete. In this search for understanding and effective strategies, the research will not be limited by the rigid boundaries of popular opinion. It may sometimes appear as though I am overstepping the very parameters I have set, but as you'll see, this is necessary for a comprehensive examination and an honest discourse.

I responded to the woman in the library with an article I just read about Dr. Ben Carson—a world renowned surgeon and son of a single Black mother—on my mind (see Ryan, 1997). I said that there are many examples of Black single mothers who are successfully raising their sons. These women often find assistance in extended family support systems (Dickerson, 1995). She said that extended family networks may have been helpful in the past but are not an integral part of life in today's Black communities. She was referring to the segregated South, where many blood relatives lived in close proximity, as did African American lawyers, doctors, teachers, business owners, the rich and poor. It was this large network of family, friends, and community that provided support and role models for children (Wilson, 1995). However, many Blacks today, for reasons, do not live in these types of settings. For example, the woman in the library lives 2000 miles away from her nearest blood relatives and hardly knows any of her multiethnic neighbors.

Many of the participants in this project live in Southern California. Some live far away from family and the familiar neighborhoods that produced the majority of today's Black leaders. Melvin Wilson, who writes extensively about the existence and success of extended Black family systems, recently spoke about the decrease in Black support systems:

Although the extended family system represents an enduring cultural value within the African American community, increasingly persistent and prevalent social and personal difficulties may now foment the demise of this valued family system. Effort must be made to avert and impede the direction of social events, because not only does the loss of the Black family threaten the African American community, but the whole American society will suffer as well. (Wilson, 1995, pp. 15–16)

When Black families live far away from family and friends, who provides support and who serves as role models for young Black males? In addition to the single mother-son dynamics, migration, desegregation, and other social pressures are negatively affecting Black families, in particular, Black males. Given the adaptability and resiliency of Black families (Hill, 1997), it will be interesting to see, as the data unfolds, how these families have recreated support systems.

Class is also an important risk factor to consider. Socioeconomic conditions often determine the supply and availability of role models in a community. When class is combined with such phenomena as migration and desegregation, finding appropriate support and role models becomes even more problematic. Consider middle-class Blacks who live in multiethnic and multicultural settings. There may be only a few Black neighbors, Black teachers and students at their schools, and even fewer Black-owned institutions. Because Black judges, ministers, teachers,

5

doctors, lawyers, and other professionals often choose to live in the suburbs, Black males in low-income neighborhoods do not have access to role models and support systems.

As I worked on this research project, my wife became pregnant. This was to be our first child. I did not know if our baby would be a boy or a girl, and I often found myself wondering if our parental responsibilities would differ based on the permutations and combinations of our genders—mine, my wife's, and the baby's. I wondered if my child would need my strengths based on my maleness and my wife's strengths based on her femaleness. Was it about the caring, spirituality, provision, and nurturing that transcended a parent's gender? Or was parenting a combination of the two? Certainly I'll be teaching my daughter valuable and esoteric lessons that are solely based on my experiences as a Black man.

Defining Masculinity and Manhood

Defining manhood and masculinity is not a simple task because our definitions change over time and cultures. However, Na'im Akbar provides a definition that has the breadth, depth, and scope to stand the test of time. He sees manhood as a process of becoming as well as an achievement. "A male is a biological creature, a boy is a creature in transition, and a man is something that has arrived to a purpose and a destiny" (1991, p. 43).

Manhood is the process and the goal, the means and the end. It involves the developmental stages and life seasons of biological males, from birth to death. Akbar's definition gives men a high goal to aspire to. For single mothers, it is a definition that can provide insight into the behaviors of their sons and guide parenting strategies.

In popular culture, however, manhood is understood as a function of a set of responsibilities, intellect, physical prowess, attitudes, and beliefs. Western culture provides the context for this Eurocentric style of manhood. This is the style of manhood most Black males seek to emulate, despite its inherent problems. In Table 2, I have listed Western-based masculine and feminine stereotypes that usually define our relationships and determine our attitudes, beliefs, and behaviors.

Table 2: Masculine and Feminine Stereotypes

Masculine stereotypes are "positive."

Feminine	Masculine
Passive	Aggressive
Dependent	Independent
Emotional	Unemotional
Does not hide emotions	Almost always hides emotions
Subjective	Objective
Easily influenced	Not easily influenced
Submissive	Dominant

Dislikes math and science	Likes math and science
Excitable in a minor crisis	Not excitable in a minor crisis
Still	Active
Not competitive	Competitive
Illogical	Logical
Domestic	Worldly
Unskilled in business	Skilled in business
Sneaky	Direct
Does not know the ways of the world	Knows the ways of the world
Feelings easily hurt	Feelings not easily hurt
Not adventurous	Adventurous
Has difficulty making decisions	Can make decisions easily
Cries easily	Never cries
Follows	Leads
Insecure	Self-confident
Powerless	Powerful
Not ambitious	Ambitious
Unable to separate feeling from ideas	Easily able to separate feelings from ideas
Vain about appearance	Uncaring about appearance
Thinks women are superior to men	Thinks men are superior to women
Does not talk freely about sex with men	Talks freely about sex with women

Feminine stereotypes are "positive."

Feminine	Masculine
Doesn't use harsh language	Uses harsh language
Talkative	Not talkative
Tactful	Blunt
Gentle	Rough
Aware of others' feelings	Unaware of others' feelings
Religious	Earthly
Interested in appearance	Not interested in appearance
Neat	Sloppy
Quiet	Loud
Needs security	Doesn't need security
Enjoys art and literature	Does not enjoy art and literature
Easily expresses tender feelings	Does not express tender feelings easily

(Broverman, 1972, p. 63)

Black Male Statistics

Pleck (1981) contends that the Western paradigm of traditional masculinity is hazardous to a man's health. Consider the following statements:

1. Aggressiveness and competitiveness cause men to put themselves in dangerous situations.

2. Emotional inexpressiveness causes psychosomatic and other health problems.
3. Men take greater risks.
4. Men's jobs expose them to physical danger.
5. Men's jobs expose them to psychological stress.
6. The male role socializes men to have personality characteristics associated with high mortality.
7. Responsibilities as family breadwinners expose men to psychological stress.
8. The male role encourages certain specific behaviors that endanger health, specifically tobacco smoking and alcohol consumption.
9. The male role psychologically discourages men from taking adequate medical care of themselves. (Pleck, 1981)

While all males may be at risk, Black male statistics are especially alarming. This issue has dominated nearly all the literature concerning Black males from 1970 to the present, and some of the statistics are listed below:

- The leading cause of death among Black males between the ages of 15 to 24 is homicide. (Center for Disease Control, 1998)
- The leading causes of death among Black males between the ages of 25 to 34 are HIV and homicide, respectively. (Center for Disease Control, 1998)
- Suicide is the third leading cause of death among young Black males ages 15–24 (Center for Disease Control, 1998)

10

- While Blacks account for 13 percent of the U.S. population, they account for greater than 50 percent of the nation's prisoners. Nearly nine of ten Black inmates are males. (U.S. Department of Justice, 1998)
- Fourteen percent of Black males are unemployed. (U.S. Bureau of the Census, 1998)
- Sixty-six percent of Black families with children under 18 are maintained by the mother. (U.S. Bureau of the Census, 1998)
- In all cities, Black males have dramatically higher suspension, expulsion, retention and drop out rates, and dramatically lower grade point averages. (Midgette & Glenn, 1993)
- Black male life expectancy is 66.1 years, compared to 73.8 years for Anglo males. (Stolberg, 1997)

Summary

It should be clear that the issue of Black mothers raising boys is not a simple one. While I absolutely agree with Haki Madhubuti's statement that "it is obvious that women cannot be replaced as mothers, nor men as fathers without serious and often detrimental disruptions to the family" (p.12), there is much to be analyzed and sifted through before we arrive at such a conclusion.

Black mother-son relationships are influenced by a host of variables and factors. Thus, it is important that the reader gains an understanding of the developmental and sociohistorical influences. We'll be discussing those influences in the next chapter. Far too many individuals engage in this dialogue merely from a personal and emotional perspective that lacks a historical context. The following chapters will provide the reader with the depth and context to more intelligently discuss this subject.

Chapter 2
Am I a Man? The Historical and Social Influences of Manhood Development

I am an invisible Man. No, I am not a spook like those who haunt Edgar Allan Poe; nor am I one of your Hollywood-movie ectoplasms. I am a man of substance, of flesh and bone, fiber in liquids—and I might even be said to possess a mind. I am invisible, understand, simply because people refuse to see me. Like the bodiless heads you see sometimes in circus sideshows, it is as though I have been surrounded by mirrors of hard, distorting glass. When they approached me they see only my surroundings, themselves, or figments of their imagination—indeed, everything and anything except me.

Ralph Ellison
Invisible Man

If you knew him you would know why we must honor him: Malcolm was our manhood, our living black manhood! This was his meaning to his people. And, in honoring him, we honor the best in ourselves...And we will know him then for what he was and is— a Prince—our own black shining Prince!— who didn't hesitate to die, because he loved us so.

Ossie Davis
Eulogy for Malcolm X
February 1965

How does a boy become a man? This may appear to be a simple question, especially when the dominant paradigm in our society suggests that manhood is achieved at the moment a male becomes a certain age. According to this model, manhood is a biological right.

Akbar's definition of manhood in the last chapter suggests that becoming a man is much more complex—at least for African American males. In African cultures, boys become men via various rites of passage rituals and programs. In America, Africans have not developed rites of passage to usher Black boys into manhood. As a result, Black boys become men according to the Western paradigm. Even so, Black manhood is negated by Western society in many ways. Like Ralph Ellison, Black men are rendered invisible. As we will explore later in this chapter, the essence of Black manhood and character is destroyed by the media. Power dynamics in the United States deny some Black men the ability to be viewed as men. This has been the Black man's problem since the beginning of African slavery in America.

It is important to note a curious, but important, omission in most "scholarly" articles concerning Black men. Excluding his ancient travels to the Americas (see Van Sertima, 1976), African American man is a recent phenomenon. He has been transformed by colonialism, imperialism, oppression, and physical and mental slavery, and thus, he must be studied in this context while keeping in mind his ancient origins. Next to the Black woman, the Black man is perhaps the oldest human creature on the face of the earth. We do him a great injustice when we present him as having his origins in slavery. W.E.B. DuBois underscores this point in his 1909 book *The Negro Family*:

> In each case an attempt has been made to connect present conditions with the African past. This is not because Negro Americans are Africans, or can trace an unbroken social history from Africa, but because there is a distinct nexus between Africa and America which, though broken and perverted, is nevertheless not to be neglected by the careful student. (p.9)

African scholars have long sought to correct the erroneous writings of Eurocentric scholars. The following works should be examined to place the Black man in a much broader historical context than has so far been done: *Black Man of the Nile* (ben-Jochannan, 1981); *African Origins of Civilization* (Diop, 1974); *Introduction to African Civilizations* (Jackson, 1970); and *The Destruction of Black Civilization* (Williams, 1987).

The Sociohistorical Dynamics of Black Manhood and Masculinity

Scholars have argued that Black men have been collectively emasculated because of the following reasons:

1. Slavery disempowered Black men and rendered them unable to protect themselves or their families.

15

2. A matriarchal system within Black communities, caused by an absent father or an "overpowering Black woman," emerged within the context of a patriarchal U.S. society that expects men to be the heads of households.

3. Economic oppression rendered Black men unable to provide for their families. Manhood and the ability to provide are inextricable in Western society.

Slavery

"Scientific work must be subdivided, but conclusions which affect the whole subject must be based on a study of the whole. One cannot study the Negro in freedom and come to general conclusions about his destiny without knowing his history in slavery." (Du Bois, 1898, p. 12)

The brutal and inhumane system of slavery in the U.S. (see Douglas, 1988) left the Black male psychologically and, in some instances, physically emasculated (Akbar, 1984). Blacks in Africa may have lived under a patriarchal system as Robert Staples suggests (1978a); however, the African male role was not respected by White owners. In fact, given the system of patriarchy in which there can be only one leader in a family—the man—by extension, there could only be one master, one power in society—the White man. Thus, the Black man became the natural target for destruction by the White male.

I agree with Del Jones (1992) that this patriarchal system, guided by White supremacy, will destroy anyone, male or female, who gets in its way of achieving and maintaining world domination and control. It is fruitless to debate who has been oppressed the most, the Black man or woman; instead, let us realize that collectively we have all been victimized by the White regime. By providing this sociohistorical context, we can discuss the issue of raising Black boys more intelligently.

Many scholars have focused on the victimization of Black women, and I encourage you to read them. However, the focus of this book is Black men. Without a doubt, Black men have been and continue to be the focus of oppression. Simple logic maintains that if you destroy the head, you destroy the body. Na'im Akbar clarifies:

> The allegory is seen throughout nature that the most certain way to destroy life is to cut off the head. From the turkey to the cow, to the man, the most immediate way to bring death to the body is to remove its head. This is especially true as a social principle. One of the things that was systematically done during slavery was the elimination of control of any emerging head or leader. Slave narratives and historical accounts are full of descriptions of atrocities brought against anyone who exemplified real leadership capability. The slave-holders realized that their power and control over the slaves was dependent upon the absence of any indigenous leadership among the slaves. (1984, p. 15)

Any Black male who wanted to stand up and be a man, *a leader*, has been isolated, killed, beaten, or ridiculed. Black manhood was clearly a threat to the patriarchy, and

17

it became dangerous to be a Black man. Moreover, out of a desire to ensure the survival of their sons, some parents prevented them from displaying any outward shows of boldness, outspokenness, and leadership, a strategy still being implemented today (Akbar, 1984, 1991). These factors contribute to the loss of Black manhood.

There are many theories on when Black males lost their manhood. The idea that Black males were emasculated during slavery is pervasive in the literature. bell hooks has a different view. She contends that slavery, especially during the early years, had little effect on African men's masculinity (1981). She confronts Staples' (1973) argument suggesting that the masculinization of African men was undermined by his inability to protect his woman. hooks writes:

> Staples' argument is based on the assumption that enslaved black men felt responsible for all black women and were demoralized because of their inability to act as protector—an assumption that has not been substantiated by historical evidence. An examination of many African societies' attitudes toward women reveals that African men were not taught to see themselves as the protectors of all black women. They were taught to assume responsibility for the particular women of their tribe or community. The socialization of African men to see themselves as the "owners" of all black women and to regard them as property they should protect occurred after the long years of slavery and as the result of bonding on the basis of color rather than shared tribal connection or language. (1981)

According to hooks, there were no cultural, social, or historical reasons for enslaved African males to feel or act responsible for enslaved African females prior to the slavery experience.

hooks' contribution to the debate primarily rests in her questioning whether African men were predisposed to view themselves as the protectors of all African women prior to their American slavery experience. She argues that Black men were not emasculated during slavery because they did not come to the Americas feeling responsible for all Black women, by writing that African male slaves began to accept the sexist Western paradigm. (Akbar, 1984).

Matriarchy

The so-called matriarchy and its offshoot, Black female headed households, is a source of tension in the literature. Four points of view are taken, which I explore below.

Absence of Black fathers. The first view posits that the absence of Black fathers from the household combined with powerful Black women leading the family causes the social ills plaguing Black males and their communities (Moynihan, 1965). The advocates of this position (e.g., Davis, 1994) contend that when fathers are absent, Black males fail to learn how to become men. (Keep in mind when examining this view that an aim of White supremacy is to present an image of a weak Black male.) Thus, they are eternal boys, and under a matriarchal system, they will never learn to be men. But Robert Staples asserts:

> Those who argue that male children can not learn the content of their masculine role make the erroneous supposition that there are no male role models available from whom those children can learn. (1978a, p. 171)

Economic oppression. Staples (1978a, 1978b) argued that it is economic oppression that deprives Black males of their manhood, not the absence of fathers in the home. Traditionally, Black males suffer inordinately high rates of unemployment. Without a source of income, they are unable to provide for their families. Being able to provide is central to being a man.

Matriarchy does not exist. The third view is found in Black feminist literature. Patricia Collins (1990, 1994) and bell hooks (1981) argue that racist scholars created the myth of the Black female matriarch to foster division within African families. Hooks maintains that there has never been at any time in the U.S. the existence of a matriarchal system because women have never held power.

> The term matriarch implies the existence of a social order in which women exercise social and political power, a state which in no way resembles the condition of black women or all women in American society. (1981, p. 71)

Multiple factors. Kunjufu (1994) points to the absence of the fathers from the home and the dearth of positive male role models in Black communities. Moreover, female-headed houscholds represent a type of power, or perhaps better stated, *influence*, in the socialization process of Black males. Wright captures the sentiments of the scholars who hold this view:

> Their teachers in the first five years of school, from kindergarten to the fourth grade are usually women. If they get in trouble, a female teacher will send them to a principal—often a woman—who will report their behavior to a female head of household…Is it no wonder that these young boys begin early either to develop an attitude of hating women or else to emulate women even to adopting their mannerisms? Neither result is desirable or acceptable.
> …Try as they may, and well meaning as they may be, women cannot teach black boys to be men. The boys need close association of legitimated Black role models, and the earlier this becomes a reality, the better adjusted the child will become. (1991, p. 22)

Wright's statement supports the argument for all-Black male schools and rites-of-passage programs led by Black male adults. The fundamental purpose of these schools and programs is to show Black males how to become Black men.

Economic Oppression

In the U.S., manhood and the ability to provide for one's family are inextricable. Because of institutional racism, Black males have been denied the role of provider (Hunter & Davis, 1994). Consequently, Black males are not viewed as men by the larger society.

According to some scholars (Hunter & Davis, 1994), this denial of manhood, combined with the Black Power Movement of the 1960s, created a new Black male psyche. Alvin Poussaint (1982) asserts:

> A fundamental change in the Afro-American male psyche occurred with the advent of the Black Power Movement in the late 1960s. A fresh, virile, sexually potent image appeared, bolstered by an assertive, more confident Black man. The Negro male became the Black male—a transformation that henceforth would never be completely safe for White society. (p. 39)

For the first time in our history in America, Black males asserted their manhood and became respected as men by society (Hunter & Davis, 1994).

This assertive, highly frustrated, angry Black male responded to oppression and explosive social events, such as the assassinations of Martin Luther King and Malcolm X, in violent ways, including the urban revolts of the 1960s. Once viewed as a political vehicle for achieving social justice, this new masculinity is now seen as pointless, dangerous, and maladaptive (Hunter & Davis, 1994). Ongoing institutional racism continues to fuel the anger of Black males, especially those who live in poor inner city communities. Often they respond according to the Western sex-role paradigm (i.e., violently) (Oliver, 1984).

Male Sex-Role Identity Development

As they embrace Western stereotypes of masculinity (see Table 2), Black males become both victims of and participants in their own destruction. These stereotypes are not necessarily the character traits that define true manhood (Akbar, 1991). Given all the dynamics within American society and the Black community itself that threatens the development of Black manhood, the question remains, Under what circumstances can a Black boy become a man?

Socialization

From the moment a child makes his or her way out of the birth canal, he/she is bombarded by environmental influences and social expectations that result in personality and behavioral divisions according to gender. From the choice of names to the type of clothes, toys, and room decor, the child is programmed to view life through a specific gender lens. Even colors are assigned to specific genders (blue for boys, pink for girls). As a boy grows up, several environmental factors act as socialization agents in the development of the male sex-role paradigm. How boys are influenced by and learn from these factors is frequently debated by psychologists and learning theorists. Three major schools of thought emerge in the discussion of the acquisition of sex-role attributes: biology, social learning, and cognition.

Biology. Sigmund Freud (1905/1972) saw sex-role development as a function of a child's biological sex. According to Freud, after a child passes through infancy, which is the same for boys and girls, the child enters the phallic period by four years of age. During the phallic period, a child has sexual desire for the opposite-sex parent. Boys covet their mothers and view their fathers as rivals (the Oedipal complex), while girls desire their fathers and view their mothers as rivals (the Electra complex). Out of a fear of his father and of castration, a boy learns to identify with his father, thus internalizing his moral characteristics and behaviors. Fearing the loss of her mother's love, a girl seeks to seal the bond by identifying with her mother, thus internalizing the moral characteristics and behaviors of the mother. According to Freud, the girl's fear of losing her mother's love is less pronounced than the boy's fear of castration; thus, girls never fully internalize the female role.

Although parents are indeed critical in sex-role development, Freud's theory is problematic because it leaves girls incomplete and it restricts the early development of children's sex roles to biology. Moreover, Freud's theory does not account for children who do not have an opposite-sex parent or who live in extended family situations where there is more than one mother present, such as Black children who may have many bloodmothers, othermothers, and grandmothers (see Collins, 1990). Freud's theories do not articulate the many complexities involving the sex-role development of Black children, specifically, Black males.

Social learning. This theory contends that sex roles are formed through socialization. The social learning theory (also called "purposive reinforcement perspective," Bandura, 1986) contends that positive and negative reinforcements are used to create sex-related behaviors or characteristics within a child. Because of the specific reinforcements boys receive from their caretakers, they become more aggressive, autonomous, and competitive than girls (Snyder and Patterson, 1986).

Cognition. This theory also contends that sex roles are formed through socialization. The cognitive perspective posits that children actively structure their experiences, categorize themselves, and classify their environment. Sex-role socialization is a function of this expansion of a child's knowledge base (Lapsley, 1990). Sex-role behaviors arise as a child seeks to identify with cues in the environment. According to the cognitive perspective, boys act aggressively, competitively, or violently because they seek to identify with other males. According to cognitive theorists Lewis and Weinraub:

1. The infant acquires knowledge about itself and at the same time, the infant acquires knowledge about others.
2. Gender and sex-role knowledge is acquired early.
3. The infant acts in a manner of like objects. (1979, p. 145)

The social learning and cognitive perspectives provide useful insight into the ways in which children process information and develop certain values, attitudes, beliefs, and behaviors.

The Family

Family is the primary agent of socialization for most infants. A male child receives information about himself and his environment through the family. Parents, especially fathers, describe and view their infants' behaviors along sex-stereotyped lines. Daughters are seen as softer and more beautiful. ("What a darling girl!" "My, she is dainty.") On the other hand, boys receive comments about their strength. ("What a strong boy!" "My, how muscular he is.") (Sigel, 1986) These perceptions are reinforced within children by the general society.

Franklin contends that the family facilitates the socialization of male children in the following ways:

1. It provides a setting whereby he can observe and learn how males are supposed to behave.
2. It provides direct and indirect tuition about the male role to a child. (1984, p. 36)

In the first example, a child observes males and females in the family as they interact with one another. Gender differences are both overtly and subtly emphasized and taught. From his observations he forms an understanding of his own role and the role of others. As a cognitive being, the male child learns that when he engages in certain behaviors he is rewarded; in the context of Western society, stereotyped characteristics and behaviors of masculinity are more often than not reinforced.

Parents

A parent's ethnic and cultural background constructs one's parenting goals, behaviors, and attitudes, and influences the sex-role development of their children. Walter Allen's study (1985) found that the child-rearing goals of Black parents differ from that of Whites. A survey that rated five of the most and least important child-rearing goals revealed that Black parents rated ambition and obedience as the most important goals, while White parents chose honesty and happiness. The different goals may be linked to culture of origin as well as to orientation to the dominant culture.

In other words, both African cultural traditions (Billingsley, 1992) and survival strategies developed during slavery are influencing Black parenting goals, practices, and traditions today. That is why Black parents raise their children to be respectful of elders (African influence) while teaching them strategies for survival in a White supremacist society (slavery influence). Most Black children have been taught to be "twice as good as the White man in order to get ahead." They have been trained to know when and how to speak to White folks. Likewise, Black children's sex roles are constructed in the context of traditional African practices and the African American defense against racism.

Extended families. The popular African proverb, "It takes a whole village to raise a child," has long been a practice of African people before it became a phrase used

27

in presidential political rhetoric. West African families have been traditionally organized around blood ties made up of adult siblings of the same sex (Sudarkasa, 1988). This core group consisted of spouses, children, and divorced siblings of the opposite sex living in connected households known as compounds (Sudarkasa, 1988). In these settings, child rearing was a collective responsibility. Child development was not linked to the characteristics of the biological parents, but through a collective effort of a community guided by a living history and cultural norms and practices.

Some scholars believe that the extended African family system was destroyed by the common slave practice of selling Africans to other plantations, thus separating family members. Instead, African families were expanded. Children taken from their biological parents on one plantation were embraced and raised by surrogate mothers, fathers, grandparents, and aunts and uncles on another plantation (Billingsley, 1992). Today, many Black children are being raised by caretakers other than their biological parents because of the collective effort of families and the community (Collins, 1994). Thus, Black children's sex-role development is influenced by multiple human and social variables.

Regarding their role as parents, *Black fathers* have long been viewed as invisible men in the social science literature (McAdoo, 1981, 1988); most of the attention has been given to mothers' roles in general. However, this focus on mothers does not include research dedicated to the Black woman's participation in the development of her son's manhood and masculinity.

The literature reveals that Black fathers are excited about becoming a parent, believe that both parents should provide child care (Hyde & Texidor, 1994), are more involved in child care than White fathers (Allen, 1985), become more involved as economic sufficiency increases (McAdoo, 1988), and want their sons to be similar to themselves in terms of parenting (Hyde & Texidor, 1994).

While there is general information about Black fathers as parents, the academic literature does not describe how Black fathers raise their sons to become men. This omission may be due to the following:

1. It is generally accepted that males naturally model their fathers and become men. This process seems so natural that it is taken for granted and not deemed worthy of study.

2. Given the fact that more than 50 percent of Black children under 18 years old now live with single mothers (Billingsley, 1992), it may be concluded that it is not necessary to examine this subject.

Obviously, Black father and son dynamics need more scholarly attention and investigation.

Black grandmothers, especially those whose own daughters are single mothers, are actively involved in the child care of their grandchildren (George & Dickerson,

1995). Although grandmothers' involvement in the affairs of their grandchildren is not new to the experience of African people, the increasing number of grandparents becoming primary caregivers is noteworthy in terms of future studies to understand the sex-role development of Black children.

In addition to the family are many other environmental and social factors influencing the sex-role development of Black male children. Many of them, especially the media, are having negative effects.

The Media

Many studies have been written concerning the effects of television, movies, radio, newspapers, magazines, comics, and music on the socialization process (Dines & Humez, 1995). These works all conclude that the mass media not only influences sex roles but class and race roles as well.

In her review of the literature, Carolyn Stroman (1991) contends that the degree to which television influences individuals is dependent upon a number of variables (see Table 3). For example, the age, sex, race, prior experience, and socioeconomic status of the individual all are important factors in calculating television's effects. Although Stroman is addressing the effects of television in particular, these variables appear to generalize across media forms and should be kept in mind when evaluating all types of media.

Movies have their greatest impact on a child when s/he identifies with one or more of the characters portrayed (Dines & Humez, 1995). Characters stimulate a child's imagination, which can lead to the expression of related feelings, needs, and desires in the real world. For the male or female that closely identifies with a character, life and the movies may become confused, causing his or her behavior and thoughts to be an imitation of what is seen on the screen. Thus viewing a violent movie may make a child with aggressive tendencies act out aggressive feelings (Comstock & Paik, 1991). Wilson adds that the sex, race, and age of the movie character positively influence the identification process. Under certain conditions, identification with characters different than the child in race, class, age, and sex occurs, especially when the child's background, cultural, ethnicity, class, etc., are sources of self-hatred (Wilson, 1978). In other words, because being Black and/or poor often carries a negative connotation, Black boys and girls seek to identify with characters that represent mainstream culture.

Table 3

Hypothesized Model for Understanding Television's

Socializing Impact

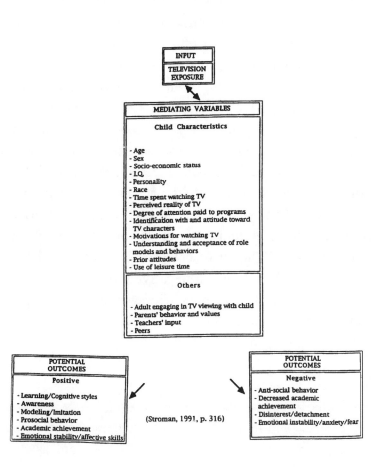

(Stroman, 1991, p. 316)

Comics. Though it may not be as pertinent today as it was in the past, comics, like movies, influence children through the identification process. An early study on comics reported that a child's interest in comics happens concomitantly with the hero stage of development occurring in late childhood (Hurlock, 1964). Boys and girls connect differently with comic books (Hurlock, 1964). Boys tend to identify with the comic book's hero. They are mostly interested in action, plots that highlight masculinity and aggression in dangerous circumstances. Comics emphasizing crime, violence, and sports appear to be the most attractive to boys. Girls, on the other hand, seem more attracted to storylines that depict women and animals, and are less interested in adventure, mystery, and thrillers (Hurlock, 1964).

A 1991 study conducted by Michael McKenna, Dennis Kear, and Randolph Ellsworth of 18,185 elementary-age students (50 percent girls) in grades 1–6, reported that at all grade levels, low-ability readers indicated, on a self-reporting checklist of six types of printed materials, that comic books were their first choice.

Deborah Chavez's 1986 study suggests that there is unequal treatment of genders in comic strips. Chavez conducted a 30-day analysis of 100 randomly selected comic strips and found that men were main characters 85 percent of the time. Only four percent of women were depicted in laborforce situations. In addition, men were shown in diverse occupations, compared to women who were bank tellers and secretaries. Most comics had White characters; Chicanos were represented only two percent of the time (no Blacks).

Characters in the comics represent certain aspects of a child's personality. These characters are in essence models for children's behavior. The characters featured in television shows and commercials intervene in the socialization process by not only providing the child with models for sex-role imitation, but also constructing paradigms for fathers, mothers, grandparents, siblings, and the community at large.

Television is an important part of life in the United States. Anthony Browder writes that:

- The average American household has at least two TV sets and one video recorder.
- The average American spends 1/5 of their lives (approximately 15 years) watching TV.
- Of the time spent viewing TV, approximately 50 minutes of each day is spent just watching commercials.

That amounts to a lifetime average of 1½ years of watching just TV advertisements. (1989, pp. 49–50)

Let us consider the impact of these viewing behaviors on children and sex-role socialization. There is evidence that infants are influenced by watching TV. Andrew Meltzoff (1988) found that infants 14 months old imitate what they see on TV. In Meltzoff's study, infants

34

observed an adult on television dismantle and put back together an object that resembled a dumbbell. The next day, when the infants were given this unfamiliar object, many of them tried to take apart and reassemble the object just as they watched on television.

Young children often confuse the make-believe on television with reality. Researchers found that three-year-old children were unable to determine if images on television sets were pictures or real, physically present beings (Flavell, Green, & Flavell, 1990). Seven and eight-year-old children also find that distinguishing reality from television characters is problematic. According to Aimee Dorr (1983), these children contend that actors wear bulletproof vests just in case the bullets are real and that actors who play married couples must be friends in real life.

In their study of children's perceptions of sex-roles and television viewing, McGhee and Frueh (1980) reveal that children in grades 1, 2, 5, and 7 who watched TV 25 or more hours per week had more stereotyped notions of males than those who were labeled as light viewers—10 or less hours per week.

Consider the study conducted by Mamay and Simpson (1981) of female roles in TV commercials. According to the researchers, men on television are depicted generally in work outside the home, as experts in mechanical and chemical products. They are catered to and pampered by their wives, and for the most part, do not participate in household chores and activities. Mamay and Simpson conclude that the women in the commercials are typecast according to three stereotypical roles: mother, housekeeper, and sexual objects. Jackson Katz contends that in commercials, the dissimilarities of males and females are both implicitly and explicitly pronounced. However, in the current era in which gender lines are more fluid, advertisers have a more difficult task stressing gender differences. Katz writes:

> Stressing gender difference in this context means defining masculinity in the opposition to femininity. This requires constantly reasserting what is masculine and what is feminine. One of the ways this is accomplished, in the image system, is to equate masculinity with violence (and femininity with passivity). (1995, p. 135)

Thus television affects socialization, and the more often it is viewed, the more influential it becomes. Wilson (1978) and Stroman (1991) write that television is not all bad because it can serve as a way for a child to acquire knowledge and can introduce new perspectives and worlds. "It is not a question of whether a child should watch TV but of balancing TV watching with other important activities" (Wilson, p. 105).

Several scholars have written about the pejorative impact of the media on Black children (e.g., Hall, 1995). They contend that negative images presented in all of the media conspire with many hours of television viewing to produce a negative effect on Black children's self-image.

36

Black children watch television on average seven to eight hours a day (Browder, 1989), as compared to 4½ hours for White children. In addition, the identification process may be heightened within Black children (Browder, 1989). Thus high viewing levels combined with the presentation of inappropriate models contributes to a variety of pathologies in the Black community, including violent behavior, alcohol and drug addiction, and sexual irresponsibility. Clearly, television may be the key element in socializing Black males according to the Western paradigm.

Consider Browder's statements about Black children and television:

- Black children tend to be more emotionally involved in the plot of TV programs.

- Black children often use TV as a substitute for other activities such as reading or interacting with other children.

- Black children tend to use TV as a source of role models. They imitate other people's behavior, dress, appearance, and speech.

- Black children use information gathered from television for guidance and direction when making career choices.

- TV provides examples of relationships with members of the opposite sex.

- TV is used as a primary source of learning and perfecting aggressive behavior.

- Black children closely identify with television characters—particularly the black characters. (1989, p. 47)

Given Black children's identification with and belief in television characters, along with the high levels of violence, sex, racism, and other negative behaviors that appear on television programs, Hutchinson (1994) and other researchers conclude that the media directly contributes to pathologies in the African community.

> You must realize that television trivializes human life by showing a murder every 57 seconds. This fact impacts directly on the high rate of black-on-black homicide. This is a cause and effect relationship. You should also realize that the high rate of teen pregnancy among blacks is directly related to the numerous programs, which feature sexual promiscuity. Few television shows provide information on sexual responsibility. (Browder, 1989, p. 48)

Given that Black children look to television for their role models, direction on making career choices, perfecting aggressive behavior, and interacting with the opposite sex (Browder, 1989), Black males are left to imitate and model maladaptive behaviors and characteristics that are pervasive in the media.

Hutchinson (1994) argues that the media overwhelmingly depicts Black men as violent criminals, clowns and buffoons, and effeminate, which is not by coincidence but is part of a larger plan by the "power structure" to eliminate Black males. Hutchinson writes that Hollywood not only participates in the assassination of Black males by presenting inappropriate and inaccurate models, but that they support Black writers, directors, and actors who engage in the same activity. He points to movies like *Boyz N the Hood*, where Black males are shown as gang bangers, drive-by shooters, and dope dealers. First a book but now a movie, *Waiting to Exhale* depicts Black males as "ugly, stupid, prisoners, unemployed, crackheads, short, liars, unreliable, irresponsible, possessive, old and set in their ways" (Hutchinson, p. 2).

Music has long been an important historical and cultural medium in African life. Music is used in ceremonial rituals and serves as a form of communication, with forces seen and unseen. In African culture, music is a healing force and is used in storytelling. Music is just as important to Africans in America today.

African music in the U.S. has greatly influenced mainstream American culture, with its spirituals, jazz, rock and roll, blues, rhythm and blues, and now rap and hip hop music, "one of the most important U.S. cultural phenomena of the last decade by many measures" (Dines & Humez, p. 1995, p. 479). On one hand, scholars (e.g., Duncan, 1994) have written about the ability of certain types of rap music to instill messages of liberation and African-centeredness, thereby raising the level of Black consciousness. On the other hand, Black community leaders have been in some cases reluctant to speak out against another style of rap music that is especially degrading to women and presents images of hyperaggressive Black males. Reluctance on speaking out against this particular type of rap music could be due to a fear of being labeled as "out of touch." Also, given the fact that media often pits Blacks against one another, many do not want to further divide African people. Nevertheless, one can only wonder how negative lyrics and terms that put down Black women affect the development of male sex roles and Black mother-son relationships.

Peer Groups

Franklin (1984) contends that males are more susceptible to peer influence because of its emphasis on Western masculinity and devaluation of feminine traits. Thus, male bonding is encouraged at earlier ages than for females. Whether in gangs, sports teams, or fraternal clubs, young boys begin to display competitiveness, aggressiveness, violent behavior, and the devaluing of femininity. It is within peer groups that young males discuss and develop thoughts, notions, and myths about sexuality (Franklin, 1988).

Franklin (1994) suggests that since Black males tend not to participate in many socializing institutions (e.g., church, school, etc.), they often look to their peer groups for definitions of masculinity. Franklin continues:

> When Black males are peer group controlled, the types of masculinities evolving generally are based on the key traits of aggressiveness, violence, competitiveness, heterosexuality, cool poses, dominance, sexism, and passivity/indifference to mainstream society. While some may feel that these traits are dysfunctional

in today's society, for many Black males, internalizing and displaying such traits are logical strategies to
follow in a society that produces, at best, men who
must develop multiple personalities in order to function reasonably well in their day-two-day activities.
(1994, p. 15)

Institutions

 Schools. Pejorative critiques of mainstream education are abundant in the literature. Mainstream education
perpetuates stereotypical sex roles for the purpose of strati-
fication and oppression (hooks, 1994). Children come to
school having already been influenced by their families,
the media, and peer groups (Ogbu, 1991), which often provides a stereotypical orientation of sex roles. These sex
roles are then reinforced through curriculum and pedagogy.
 Religious institutions in the U.S. have always
played an important role in socialization (Stearns, 1990).
Religious books such as the Holy Bible and the Holy
Qur'an both covertly and overtly present a model for sex
roles. Explicitly, these books define the male as the leader
or head of his wife and family. Implicitly, women are
projected as evil in nature, which is why they must be con-
trolled by a human male and a male deity. The Holy Bible
has had the strongest religious and moral influence on
Western society. Its institutions, laws, and customs are
strongly influenced by Christian theology. Thus, Christian ideas about sex roles impact not only Christians but
everyone living in Western society—including Black male
children.

Religion and spirituality have great historical significance to Black families and communities. Historically, Black churches and Black families were indistinguishable as they forged a social, political, spiritual, sexual, and economic agenda.

> The Black church and the African-American family co-joined as the center of Black community life. Our sense of African spirituality dictated that the avenues and arenas of social intercourse and human development were guided by the oneness and connection of the spiritual and physical world. (Nobles, Goddard, Cavil, & George, 1987, p. 84)

Currently, the Black church represents a significant part of Black life, with more than 23 million Blacks as members of Christian institutions alone (Billingsley, 1992). Yet, it has been well documented that the majority of these congregations are made up of Black women (Kunjufu, 1995). Black church life must be considered in our discussion about Black male sex role development and the relationship between mothers and sons. Most Black males (in general and in this present study) went to church as children, and their mothers still attend regularly even if they currently do not.

Women As Socializing Agents

It is clear that in the United States, men control the resources and, thus, they hold the majority of power (Bush,

42

1995). Nevertheless, women have some control over males in society. Pleck (1976) contends that women in the U.S. have masculinity-validating power. For example, some women play the "damsel in distress" role because they believe it will make men feel more like "men," despite the fact that there may be no truth to the distressed situation. In other words, women sometimes play along with men in the game of boosting male masculinity. Males and females have been practicing this game in the home and social environment for millennia, and they have become experts.

Summary

We return to the main question of this chapter: Have Black males achieved manhood? First we looked at the many social influences on the development of Black manhood. Franklin (1984) and Poussaint (1982) propose that Black males became men in the 1960s as they began to assert themselves under the impetus of the Black Power Movement. Clearly, this assertion is judging manhood through the lens of a Western paradigm. Franklin and Poussaint ignore African notions of manhood—the synthesis of male and female roles, which were and are a part of Black men's characteristics (Roberts, 1994). They contend that Black males did not become men until they exhibited the aggressive characteristics of Western masculinity and manhood. Therefore, through this lens, some Black males have become men because they have acquired the traditional Western concept of male sex roles.

At first glance, it may seem that those individuals who propose an African-centered paradigm of manhood were guilty of Franklin and Poussaint's conclusion that Black males had not become Black men, especially before 1965. Those who look at the question through the lens of an African-centered framework readily posit that Black males never did become men (e.g., Akbar, 1991). It appeared that these scholars had omitted the recognition of men such as Nat Turner, Marcus Garvey, and Paul Robeson, who are excellent examples of African manhood. However, further investigation reveals that these scholars are not talking about the individual, because there are millions of Black males who represent fine examples of African manhood; they are referring to the collective. They contend that collectively we have not gained our manhood, and that we will only obtain it through freedom and independence.

Chapter 3
Understanding Black Motherhood

Our growing up without a father put a heavy burden on my mother. She didn't complain—at least not to us—and she didn't feel sorry for herself. She tried to carry the whole load, and somehow I understood what she was doing. No matter how many hours she had to be away from us at work, I knew she was doing it for us. That dedication and sacrifice made a profound impression on my life.

Abraham Lincoln once said, 'All that I am or ever hope to be, I owe to my mother.' I'm not sure I want to say it quite like that, but my mother, Sonya Carson, was the earliest, strongest, and most impacting force in my life.

Ben Carson, M.D.
Gifted Hands

The Black woman in the South who raises sons, grandsons, and nephews had her heartstrings tied to a hanging noose.

Maya Angelou
I Know Why the Caged Bird Sings

The literature is saturated with the negative effects of single-mother households on children (e.g., Parish, 1991). Furthermore, the research suggests that these father-absent households have a more harmful effect on male rather than female children (e.g., Hetherington, 1991). Although a body of work is emerging that is changing old pejorative views of single mothers, especially the much maligned single Black mother (e.g., Dickerson, 1995), there is still quite a gap in what we know about not only single Black mother-son relationships, but also married Black mother-son relationships.

Images of Black Mothers

Black feminist Patricia Collins (1990, 1994), along with other scholars, contends that most of what is written about Black mothers is stereotypical and inaccurate. In addition, Black mothers are often studied against the nuclear family model which, as we will see, excludes many important social dynamics influencing the development of Black children (Sudarkasa, 1988, 1993). Collins' critique will help us study Black mothers from a more accurate, culturally relevant perspective. It is my hope that the voices of Black mothers and data collected in this study will contribute to this emerging scholarship.

The stereotypes most often used to describe Black mothers are the following: mammy, matriarch, and "superstrong." Before we discuss the problems inherent with these stereotypes, let us define our terms.

Mammy. The mammy is a completely loyal and docile servant, mothering White children and serving White families. Mammies receive little compensation for their work, and they gladly accept their inferior status. Many of the old Black movies featured mammies.

46

Matriarch. Bette Dickerson (1995) distinguishes between the term matriarchy and matrifocality. A matriarch is a woman who is dominant over males and children. Matrifocality refers to mother-centeredness:

> In contrast, dominance is not a precondition for a matrifocal family system. Rather, it is a unit held together by the extended line of female kin: mother, daughters, and their children pooling resources and often sharing a household. (p. xv)

Superstrong. The superstrong Black mother is the woman who does everything and is everything to everyone. She shoulders the responsibilities of the family and community often single-handedly. According to Collins:

> By claiming that Black women are richly endowed with devotion, self-sacrifice, and unconditional love—the attributes associated with the archetypal motherhood—Black men inadvertently foster a different controlling image for Black women, that of the 'superstrong' Black mother. (1990, p. 116)

Both mammy and matriarchal images of Black mothers are held by White men and women (Collins, 1990). In *Black Macho and the Myth of the Superwoman*, Michele Wallace offers a description of the Black woman as superwoman, which is tantamount to what Collins calls "superstrong":

> [Black women are] of inordinate strength, with an ability for tolerating an unusual amount of misery

and heavy, distasteful work. This woman does not have the same fears, weaknesses, and insecurity as other women, but believes herself to be and is, in fact, stronger emotionally then most men. Less of a woman in that she is less "feminine" and helpless, she is really more of a woman in that she is the embodiment of Mother Earth, the quintessential mother with infinite sexual, life-giving, and nurturing reserves. In other words, she is a Superwoman. (1991, p. 107)

Black men often perceive Black women as "superstrong." Adding to the pressure that this image creates, Elizabeth Sparks (1996) contends that Black mothers are now "Super/Essence" women, highly educated and professional. She writes:

The Super/Essence woman is expected to be a supportive, and at times submissive, partner to her spouse, a devoted mother who is actively involved in her children's lives, while also being aggressive, competent, and career-focused in her professional life. She must be able to create and maintain a viable marriage, while also being prepared to care for herself and her children alone if necessary. (1996, p. 74)

Black superwoman images promote standards of achievement that may be unrealistic. Sparks (1996) says that where some Black mothers succeed, far more are wounded by an oppressive society that hurts women in general and Black women in particular.

Also problematic is the designation of "mothering" as the sole responsibility of one Black mother. Before, during, and after slavery, the appellation of mother in West Africa has represented an extensive network of women collectively providing child care (Sudarkasa, 1988). By only examining the role of bloodmothers in raising Black children, researchers have captured only a portion of mothering influences. It is not necessarily an incorrect research framework to give primacy to the role of bloodmothers, as this research project will do. It is unjust, however, to present research that only examines the role of Black bloodmothers as a complete explanation for the development of Black children.

The matrifocal, or mother-centered, model seems to best fit the parenting styles of Black mothers. Within Black communities, one can find women-centered networks where bloodmothers and other mothers provide child care across blood or biological ties (Collins, 1990, 1994). A Black child being raised within this framework may have more than one mother in addition to the biological mother. This practice can be traced to Africa. Contrary to the belief that slavery destroyed African culture (Frazier, 1966), Black women-centered child care networks represent a very important manifestation of a collective responsibility paradigm that has existed for centuries in West Africa (McAdoo, 1988). Research that does not account for these woman-centered networks when assessing the influence of Black motherhood on the development of children (specifically, Black males) may generate incomplete data and inaccurate conclusions.

Demographics of Black Single Mothers

Herbert Gutman (1976) notes that contrary to popular scholarship, two-parent families were in the majority during slavery. Female-headed households arose primarily due to two circumstances: (1) a husband was killed or sold to another plantation or (2) an unmarried mother, whose children were often conceived in rape by a slave master (Burgess, 1995), had cabins built for her.

Billingsley (1992) describes Black family life during the hundred years between the end of slavery and the end of World War II as stable. From 1890–1960, divorce was rare; the percentage of two-parent households with children held steady at about 80 percent. Although Billingsley does not state so explicitly, he seems to infer a correlation between the low number of well-paying jobs for undereducated Black men in the 1970s to the decreasing percentage of two-parent households. In 1960, the percentage of Black two-parent households with children was 78 percent; in 1970 it was 64 percent, in 1980, 48 percent, and in 1990, 39 percent. The percentage of single-parent households with children under 18 rose from 21.9 percent in 1960 to 54.8 percent in 1990 (see Table 1) (U.S. Bureau of the Census, 1991).

A significant body of literature postulates mother-only families produce harmful effects in children. According to this literature, children of single-mother families have higher rates of poverty, school drop out, delinquency, school absenteeism, divorce, and drug and alcohol abuse, in addition to poorer academic achievement. The absence of a male in the household is usually cited as the cause (Wright, 1991). However, there are other factors that challenge this perspective. More than half of Black single-parent families live in poverty. Suzanne Randolph (1995) writes that it is not the father's absence that causes negative effects; it is the lack of another income. The work of Vonnie McLoyd, Toby Jayaratne, Rosario Ceballo, and Julio Borquez (1994) also points to the primacy of economics.

Niara Sudarkasa (1993) argues that scholars, policy makers, and the popular media have traditionally been confused and misinformed about Black single mothers as heads of households. According to Sudarkasa (1993), programs designed to support female-headed households must be founded on a clear understanding of the development, structure, and function of female-headed households. Only then will we be able to make an accurate assessments of Black mother-son relationships.

The following six points provide an insightful perspective on Black female-headed households:

1. A key to understanding contemporary African American family structure, whether headed by women, by men, or by couples, is a knowledge of the earlier structure of African extended families out of which they evolve. It is particularly important to understand that as these African-derived extended families evolved in America, they embraced households headed by single parents, most of whom were women, as well as households headed by married couples.

2. Female-headed households are not all the same. They differ in terms of the dynamics of their formation and their functioning.
3. Marital stability and family stability are not one and the same. Female-headed households have been and can be stable over time.
4. There are demographic and socioeconomic reasons why many African American female-headed households are now and have always been a predictable and acceptable form of household organization.
5. There is a need to appreciate that women may be primary providers and heads of households in families when both parents are present as well as in situations where they are the only parent in the home.
6. It is necessary to dispute the notion that female-headed households are the main cause of the deplorable conditions of poverty, crime, and hopelessness found among blacks in many inner cities. (Sudarkasa, 1993, p. 82)

Historically, in some regions of the United States, particularly the South, Black living arrangements resembled African compounds; co-residential extended families were the norm. Black families usually built houses near each other on commonly owned land. Clusters of households headed by couples or by single women could be found in the South before Blacks began to lose control over most of the land they acquired after slavery. This proximity in residence provided opportunities for collective child rearing, financial support, caring for elders, and offering shelter to family members in need. Consequently, many single mothers found support in these collective community and household structures.

Unfortunately, extended family networks eroded due to migration and desegregation. Sudarkasa notes that poverty threatens the survival of these family networks with a particularly negative impact on female-headed households. Yet, these households would be in worse condition today if it were not for the continued existence of extended family support systems.

Sudarkasa stresses that we must understand the diversity in formation and function of female-headed households. Age and previous marital status are factors that need to be considered as we engage this particular family dynamic. For instance, households headed by young, never-married females may function very differently from households headed by widows, divorced, and separated women.

Sudarkasa hypothesizes that the recent and steady rise in Black female-headed households since the 1950s is due to a change in residential patterns more so than a rise in teenage pregnancy. Until 1950, most young and unmarried mothers lived with their mothers, grandmothers, parents, grandparents, and other relatives, a fact that went undetected by census counters when counting households. The decrease in these multigenerational living arrangements naturally caused an increase in the accountability of single mothers as they began to move into their individual households.

We must also comprehend the difference between marital stability and family stability. Sudarkasa contends that a divorce or separation does not necessarily denote an abatement in family support systems. So-called father-absent households still enjoy male role models and financial and emotional support from fathers, uncles, and other males. Yet, Sudarkasa cites unemployment as a cause of deteriorating male support.

Sudarkasa posits that female-headed households have been, and are, an accepted or "legitimate" form of family organization in Black communities. Historically, Blacks understood that some women had to conceive children without husbands if they were going to have children. Like their ancestors, Africans throughout the Diaspora and from the Continent put a high value on having children. Thus, the negative stigma sometimes felt by many White women for having children out of wedlock is not mirrored by Black women in similar circumstances.

There are certain social circumstances that exacerbate the phenomenon of single mothers. For example, the declining pool of available Black men affects this dynamic. Sudarkasa writes that some males respond to this unequal sex ratio by having multiple marriages and/or common-law living arrangements. Other men remain married as they engage in relations with other women, which often produces single mothers. These points must be taken into account if we are going to understand the full spectrum of Black single motherhood.

Sudarkasa articulates the need to clarify the role of women as co-providers or sole providers in households where both husbands and wives are present. The literature has assumed male leadership whenever a husband is present; therefore, female-headed households with a male spouse present have been ignored by scholars. Nonetheless, un-employment of Black males has caused the existence of two-parent households where women are sole providers.

Sudarkasa's last point brings us back again to one of the major issues in this project. She strongly asserts the need to destroy the myth that female-headed households are the cause for deplorable conditions that affect many Blacks. A study conducted by Reginald Clark (1983) addresses this concern.

The style or quality of parenting a child receives is a strong challenge to the theory suggesting that absent Black fathers cause pathologies in Black children. Clark used ethnographic interviewing to study the families of high- and low-achieving 12th graders. The families had the same income levels and lived in Chicago housing projects. The families fell into four categories:

1. Two-parent families with at least one high-achieving 12th grade child;
2. One-parent families with at least one high-achieving 12th grade child;
3. Two-parent families with at least one low-achieving 12th grade child;
4. One-parent families with at least one low-achieving 12th grade child. (Clark, 1983, p. 18)

Clark found that single parents and married parents of high-achieving 12th grade children had distinctive

55

parenting characteristics and behaviors when compared to single parents and married parents with low-achieving children (see Table 4). Parents of high-achievers clearly have a set of high expectations for their child's schooling and future goals, which is combined with the ability to provide consistency in enforcing boundaries and rules. Conversely, parents of low-achieving children provided inconsistent environments along with low expectations, obfuscated family roles, and little school involvement.

Table 4

A Comparison of the Quality of Success-Producing Patterns in Homes of High Achievers and Low Achievers

High Achievers	Low Achievers
1. Frequent school contact initiated by parent	Infrequent school contact initiated by parent
2. Child has had some stimulating, supportive school teachers	Child has had no stimulating, supportive school teachers
3. Parents psychologically and emotionally calm with child	Parents in psychological and emotional upheaval with child
4. Students psychologically and emotionally calm with parents	Students less psychologically and emotionally calm with parents
5. Parents expect to play major role in child's schooling	Parents have lower expectation of playing role in child's schooling

56

6. Parents expect child to play major role in child's schooling	Parents have lower expectation of child's role in child's schooling
7. Parents expect child to get post-secondary training	Parents have lower expectation that child will get post-secondary training
8. Parents have explicit achievement centered rules and norms	Parents have less explicit achievement-centered rules and norms
9. Students show long-term acceptance of norms as legitimate	Students have less long-term acceptance of norms
10. Parents establish clear, specific role boundaries and status structures with parents as dominant authority	Parents establish more blurred role boundaries and status structures
11. Siblings interact as organized sub-group	Siblings are a less structured, interactive subgroup
12. Conflict between family members is infrequent	Conflict between some family members is frequent
13. Parents frequently engage in deliberate achievement-training activities	Parents seldom engage in deliberate achievement-training activities
14. Parents frequently engage in implicit achievement-training activities	Parents engage less frequently in implicit achievement-training
15. Parents exercise firm, consistent monitoring and rules enforcement	Parents have inconsistent standards and exercise less monitoring of child's time and space

| 16. Parents provide liberal nurturance and support | Parents are less liberal with nurturance and support |
| 17. Parents defer to child's knowledge in intellectual matters | Parents do not defer to child in intellectual matters |

(Clark, 1983, p. 200)

Black Single Mothers and Male Children

Given economic conditions and parenting styles, the question remains, Are boys at a greater risk than girls in single-mother households? The literature is inconclusive, however, Suzanne Randolph (1995) writes that Black male teens in single-mother households may be overwhelmed in trying to fulfill the role of an absent father.

There is an old adage, "Mothers raise their daughters and love their sons." Randolph contends that this method of parenting may have trained boys during early post slavery years to be less aggressive and thus less prone to racist attacks. However, in today's social climate of unemployment, drugs, mis-education, and under-education, this method is maladaptive. We must address the notion that mothers are responsible for producing less aggressive males simply because they are women.

A Review of Black Mother-Son Studies

Forcey's (1987) and King and Mitchell's (1990, 1991) studies were conducted by women who have male children. They admitted to personalizing their research and, especially in the case of King and Mitchell, infused themselves in the study.

Not surprisingly, in the introduction of these studies these authors bemoan the lack of academic research concerning mother-son relationships. However, I was astonished by Forcey's statement that this topic was unpopular in other arenas as well.

By and large, the mother-son relationship is not a favorite among scholars and academics. Even I do not speak often about my sons, nor do my feminist friends and colleagues. This is strange given the fact that we speak of almost everything else—husbands, loves, fathers, and especially daughters and our own mothers. Forcey contends that women have been silenced by Freudian psychology that promotes the idea of sexual feelings between mothers and sons.

Recognizing the dearth of information in the social sciences, King and Mitchell turned to Black literature, where they found relationships between mothers and sons played out in novels, stories, and poems written by Black men. They juxtaposed the literature with data collected from group conversations with seven Black mothers, including themselves, friends, and neighbors. Using semi-structured interviews, the following questions were asked:

1. What have you done to protect your son(s) from society's hostile forces?
2. What have you taught your son(s) of honesty, loyalty, compassion, faith, and responsibility?

3. What have you taught your son(s) of reciprocity, difference, mutuality, and spirit?
4. What have you taught your son(s) of family background, secrets, and family lore? (Forcey, 1987)

Forcey used opened-ended telephone interviews (conversations, she admits) to "find out things about mothers of sons that cannot be otherwise discovered, things like feelings, thoughts, and intentions" (p. 8). One hundred and fourteen women were interviewed by Forcey and two graduate students, also mothers of sons. Examples of interview questions are not included in this study aside from background data (age, family, class, religion, race, ethnicity, education, employment history, marital status, number, age, and sex of children). Only nine percent of the participants interviewed were women of color. Forcey accounted for three variables when collecting the data.

1. The women were divided into five age categories: 18–25; 26–35; 36–45; 46–55; 56–75.
2. The women were separated according to whether or not the mother was, had been, or intended to be employed outside of the home.
3. The women were categorized as to whether they were married, had been, or were intending to be, to the father of their son(s).

King and Mitchell provide only a few of the participants' demographic data, however, Forcey does explain in more depth how certain demographics can influence the mother-son relationship. Neither study accounted for these variables in their conclusions, which resulted in a homogenous presentation of the participants. In other words, economic level, race, age, marital status, and other variables that are known to influence mother-son relationships were not incorporated in their theoretical paradigm. This is a fundamental shortcoming of these studies.

Nevertheless, Forcey provides insight into the complexity of women's feelings concerning their sons. And although their focus was not on how Black women raise their boys to become men, King and Mitchell ended up providing examples of how this process may take place between Black mothers and their sons. Both studies discuss motherhood as a Catch-22 situation, meaning mothers are "damned if they do and damned if they don't." In their interviews with Black mothers, both studies uncovered a tremendous amount of guilt held by mothers of sons.

According to Forcey:

> ...Freud, his followers, practically every biographer of famous men, most social scientists, and literary figures too, tell us that behind every conqueror, every hero, is the responsible mother, they usually describe her as overinvolved, overwhelming, and smothering. In contrast we are told that behind every vain, hypersensitive, invidious, cruel, violent, schizophrenic, paranoid, sexually deviant, narcissistic, overachieving, or merely unfulfilled male of whatever age there is that same responsible mother. (1987, p.1)

The Black mothers in King and Mitchell's study felt they were in a no-win situation. These Black mothers want to protect their sons from a cold and racist world, yet they know they must teach their sons how to survive in the world—another Catch-22. Consequently, guilty feelings arise. They wonder if they have overprotected or underprotected their Black sons. Guilt in Forcey's study was mostly associated with mothers feeling as though they have not lived up to the high expectations of society.

Manhood and masculinity were not the subjects of King and Mitchell's study, so they did not provide definitions for these terms. However, they discussed the challenges they encounter in raising their own sons, i.e., raising their boys to manhood. From an examination of key words in the interview questions, I surmise that the researchers consider the following to be important in developing Black manhood: reciprocity, mutuality, strength, honesty, loyalty, compassion, and faith.

What have you taught your son(s) of family background, secrets, and family lore? This question yielded the clearest and most telling examples of how these Black women are raising their sons to become men. These mothers talked to their sons about their fathers, grandfathers, and uncles, providing them with examples of how similar men have persevered through difficult situations while maintaining their dignity, strength, and pride. According to King and Mitchell, stories about ancestors reinforce family values and help sons overcome situations of hopelessness that can exist in an anti-African society. I believe that the Black men in these stories become role models of manhood and masculinity.

Finding other examples of how these Black women raise their sons becomes problematic because the participants' responses to the other questions tended to focus on the ways in which their sons did not live up to the prescribed components of manhood (e.g., honesty, reciprocity, and loyalty) and the women's guilty feelings. In other words, instead of discussing how they taught their sons, these mothers talked about how they felt when their sons were dishonest, disloyal, and irresponsible. King and Mitchell offer other insights into the feelings of Black mothers, but fail to address the question central to this research proposal: Can Black mothers raise our sons to become men?

Summary

This chapter has helped us configure a critical lens to view and analyze this study by deconstructing various issues surrounding Black mothers. First and foremost, blaming single Black mothers for the deplorable conditions facing Black males should be relinquished, abandoned, and forgotten. We have discovered that economic conditions, support systems, availability of positive male role models, and the quality of parenting are perhaps more salient factors in determining the outcome of Black single motherhood.

Consequently, this study must address issues centered around this adage that was unresolved in the literature: "Mothers raise their daughters and love their sons." We must also strive to engage this popular sentiment: "Try as they may, and well-meaning as they may be, women cannot teach Black boys to be men." If any of these statements have merit we must find out why or why not as we engage our central question: How do Black mothers raise their sons to become Black men?

Other more specific questions guide this present study:

1. Do barriers exist, such as ones' biological sex, lack of experiences, or other unforeseen hindrances, that render women incapable or more disadvantaged than men in being able to raise Black sons successfully?

2. What characteristics do successful Black mothers posses that help them raise their sons?

3. Are the mothers knowledgeable about issues that are seen as being unique or important to Black males or males in general such as sexuality and surviving in a society that is particularly hostile towards African men?

4. What goals do Black mothers have for their sons' masculine development? In other words, how do the mothers define Black manhood and masculinity?

5. Are family and extended family support systems part of the lives of most single Black mothers and their sons?

6. What happens to Black males who do not have a father in the home?

Chapter 4
Solve for X: Black Women + Black Boys = X

The death of Betty Shabazz last summer from injuries she sustained in a fire set by her grandson filled us all with horror. Beyond that, it gave special urgency to a debate that has raged in our communities for some time now—the question of how to raise good men when, according to the U.S. Census, some 91 percent of African-American boys do not have a father in the home. Is a father's presence necessary? What standards should we have for fatherhood in our community? And how can we raise boys into the kind of men we need for the twenty-first century?

Essence Magazine
November 1997

In the beginning God created the heaven and the earth. And the earth was without form, and void; and the darkness was upon the face of the deep. And the Spirit of God moved upon the face of the waters. And God said, Let there be light: and there was light.

Genesis 1:1–3

The true worth of a race must be measured by the character of its womanhood.

Mary McLeod Bethune
"A Century of Progress of Negro Women,"
1935

65

I posed the questions *Essence* raised and more as I interviewed 27 Black mothers and many of their sons. In this chapter, I will share the insights, fears, and strategies of Black mothers with sons. In the first part of this chapter we will pay particular attention to the issues of "how to raise boys" and defining "good men." I will present a working model of Black manhood created from the participants' insights about manhood, masculinity, and "good men." We will explore the lessons, concepts, and strategies Black mothers use to rear their sons to achieve the attributes of manhood. But first we will examine the mothers themselves—their characteristics, attributes, and knowledge base regarding the social, historical, and political dynamics of being Black and male in the United States.

In the final part of this chapter, I will juxtapose issues and concepts from the literature with data from this study. I will explore issues such as the existence and function of othermothers, extended family support systems, male role models, the premature role of young males as "the man" of the household, and the provider role. Many of these issues appear in the literature as assertions with little research to support them, or they rely on outdated sources. Thus, we will analyze how this data either supports these issues, concepts, and dynamics, or negates them.

Attributes of Black Mothers in Respect to Raising Sons

If a person is unable to accomplish a task, there must be a reason. If Black mothers are unable to raise their boys to manhood, as Holland (1991) and others suggest, there must be a reason. Some deficiency must exist within Black women. Yet, as I scoured the literature, I could not find any single deficiency that rendered them so incompetent. In fact, as I interviewed the 27 mothers, I found the opposite to be true. Although no single attribute emerged as dominant in characterizing Black mothering styles, I found that Black mothers have at their disposal a wide range of abilities, from the traditional female ones, such as nurturing and patience, to traditional male ones, such as strength and resiliency (Schoenberg, 1993). Here is a mother on being a nurturer:

Mrs. Waters, mother of a son (32), and a daughter (25).
I nurtured all children—that's one great characteristic I've been told I have. I can't see it, but that's what others have said. I am a very caring person even with my students.

Mrs. Walton, mother of sons ages 31, 30, 21, and a daughter 19, says that she's a good listener and observer. She believes that this quality is unique to her as a mother and distinguishes her from her husband.

That is a very important key. Just listening. Sometimes it's not always about having answers. Sometimes you have to listen to what is being said. I think that is the part that is different between my husband and I as far as communication with the kids. I am regarded as the one who will listen and not be so judgmental. They have gotten comfortable with this.

> [Also] I consider myself to be very observant and just being a parent you notice relationships between parent and child and behaviors in other kids that you don't necessarily like that you can point out to show your child what you like or don't like.

Below two mothers acknowledge several qualities, such as patience and justice, but the most important is spirituality.

Mrs. Miller, mother of a son (29).

Without a doubt, two things come to mind, my spiritual framework, that's a real important aspect because in that spiritual framework I learned justice, how to be a just parent. I think a lot of parents can be loving parents but not necessarily just. I believe justice is really important and trying to call the call right without destroying the child in the process, that's been really important.

Mrs. George, mother of two sons (28, 25) and two daughters (31, 30).

Patience was one, the thing you really need in raising any children or any child. A strong spiritual background, one of being honest with your children as far as raising them. Being a trustworthy and responsible person.

Mrs. White, mother of two sons (20, 14) and two daughters (24, 10) adds responsibility to the list of qualities Black mothers have to help them raise their sons:

> Just a sense of responsibility I guess. That's all I can say, it's just imbedded in me. I was the responsible one of the group when we were growing up. If my mother wanted something done, she knew who to come to. That is what I try to tell my kids, be responsible for people to know they can depend on you.

Economic factors and sometimes marital status (Randolph, 1995) can influence the mother's ability to be consistently present for her children. Ms. Evers, a single mother of 8-year-old twin sons and a 5-year-old son underscores the advantage of economic stability:

> …That I have a well paying job, that helps! That I started teaching before I had them, so I had a car, a place to live, I had a job, and then I had some twins. You can make it otherwise, but I was somewhat in place before they came and that was helpful.

Mrs. Black, a widow, was challenged economically; however, despite her family's income level, she contends that she was always "there for her children." Mrs. Black, who has sons ages, 47, 44, 40, and 36 and daughters ages 52, 40, and 37 (two sons and one daughter are stepchildren) gives us a sense of her economic circumstances and of another personal trait: consistency.

69

They were going to have a concert one night, so they were in here, Candace on the clarinet, Steve on the saxophone, he played with Dr. Hollaway at Cal Poly, they were just practicing. I can tell you I didn't have a pair of shoes to put on, to go out that night to go to the school to see them. I didn't tell them but I told them later. I had a pair of tennis shoes, they were probably worn tennis shoes that weren't very popular then, they weren't even cute. I told some kind of lie on why I could not go to their program that night. So that's how poor we were.

[Nevertheless,] I think being the person I am, I think them seeing me, when I was raising my kids, they could always say, 'She was always here.' You know how kids come home and the parent wasn't there till late in the evening. See, my husband came home late in the evening but I was always here. They had a time for dinner, a time for everything, I guess that's the reason I stayed at the job that I have all these years. They say, 'you never went anywhere else?' But it was conducive to my family and me because by the time my youngest child was up in the second grade, we could walk to school together. I'm going to work, they're going to school. I got home before them so that gave them no room for saying 'I could go to Sally's house and I don't have to be home till 6:30 p.m. because Mom won't be there.' I was here and seeing me doing the things I did might have molded them too.

Moving toward more traditionally masculine traits (Schoenberg, 1993), Mrs. Price, with two sons ages 8 and 25, adds strength to the list. Mrs. Price, who was a single mother for most of her oldest son's life, was at times inconsistent as a parent; however, she does not attribute her inconsistency to her economic status or to being single. Rather, this condition was due to a certain lifestyle, which changed because of personal and spiritual growth and maturity.

> ...Being strong. I learned from my older son, I learned from Leonard. When I had Leonard I was a junior in college, got married, 20 years old, had him then his dad and I divorced and I raised him. So I had to be kind of a mom and a dad, although I couldn't never be a dad, but I had to perform two functions as a bread winner and then as a mother in the home also. I think I learned from that to be strong and be consistent, consistency that's one thing. Being strong and consistent, meaning being clean, meaning know how to have a spirit of discernment. When you know somebody is not right you know you don't want to put that around your child and you don't want to be around that so being a strong woman, being consistent, being able to take care of him, that spirit of discernment, and just trying to live a wholesome life. Not saying I'm perfect but just trying to live a wholesome life. I learned from my younger days.

Other mothers discuss being strong and resilient as key attributes of their personality. Two mothers assert that these are the qualities that their sons will learn from them:

Mrs. Ross, mother of a son (1 month).
I am a strong Black woman and I think that is something. That is a quality within myself that he can see, that he will be able to see. No matter what you

go through in your past it's not an excuse for you to totally mess up your future. He will be able to see that in his mom.

Ms. Jones, mother of a son (12) and a daughter (10).
You don't fail if you try. I try to teach him that if he tries and learns then he gains something from that even if he doesn't get the desired outcome. I do what I have to do. I want us to survive.

Mrs. Owens, mother of a son (1) and a daughter (4).
He will be able to see that I am not a quitter. I push—real brief—I was pregnant in my teenage years but I had not finished high school and so all my girl friends around me they wound up getting pregnant too and they quit, they dropped out of school and I said, 'I'm not going to do that.' But then when that time came it got really hard, and I was behind in my education and so they had given me options to do home study, and so I said, 'I'll do that' and that was my way out of school. Then I said, 'No, I'm not going to take advantage of this.' This is showing that I could be independent, get my work done, and it came that I did my independent home study and I completed it my same year. I wasn't late, I wasn't able to walk with my general class but with other classmates that had gone through the same thing or something like that. I pushed on, I was up till 4 in the morning, hitting my books and that was very motivational for me to do that. He'll be able to see that I am not a quitter.

The last attribute I'll present speaks to Black mothers' awareness and knowledge-base about issues germane to the lives of Black males (discussed in the next section). These women maintain that their awareness, concern for, understanding, and love of Black men is, in fact, an attribute they possess that is essential to their ability to raise Black boys.

Ms. Green, mother of two sons (27, 20).
A love for Black men. I really believe that has helped me a lot. An awareness of what goes on with Black men in our society. A struggle to strive, to hang in to the end with my sons. I don't want them to ever have to be a part of the statistics in this country. I think the thing that keeps me going the most is not just a love for my sons but a love for Black men period. I think Black men really have had a struggle and don't fit in any place in this society, even less than Black women. That in itself gives me a lot of inner strength to try not to allow my sons to feel as much of that as possible. That motivates me a lot.

Ms. Homes, mother of a son (10) and a daughter (9).
A good memory [laughs], remembering what it was like growing up for me, knowing and seeing how I was parented and basically having a good memory. Being educated. Being motivated, knowing how society is and not wanting my son to be persecuted.

From this section, we find that Black women have several attributes and qualities that cover the continuum of traditional masculine and feminine characteristics. In terms of marital or income status, no patterns emerge. Both married and single mothers with several ranges in income levels equally report qualities that cover traditional masculine and feminine characteristics. We are beginning to see that contrary to the studies, Black women who have certain attributes *can* raise their sons.

Do Black Mothers Know the Time?

How does one prepare for something, such as a fight, if s/he does not know what s/he is up against or who the opponent is? How would a parent, mentor, or teacher help a child successfully negotiate life without knowing some of the challenges children face? More to the point, can Black mothers successfully raise their sons without knowing the "time," that is, without understanding White cultural hegemony and its historical, social, political, spiritual, and psychological effects on Black males?

We will use the following five categories to explore Black mothers' awareness and beliefs of the challenges that are specific to growing up Black and male in the United States:

1. The general structure of society and White cultural hegemony.
2. The negative stereotyping of Black males.
3. A debilitating and impotent educational system that miseducates Black males.

4. Black males having to work twice as hard as White males to achieve in life.
5. Finding viable male role models.

We will discover that "self-esteem" and "self-concept" are common themes in these categories.

These Black mothers perceive American society to be anti-Black male and, in essence, anti-African. The following dialogue underscores Black mothers' awareness of historical circumstances and its connection to Black males in society.

Ms. Homes: I think that as a Black male things have happened in the past and are still strong influential in the present

Interviewer: Such as?

Ms. Homes: How we were brought to America in the first place. How traditionally Black males have been treated as far as being able to be heads of their households, educationally wise how they have been perceived in the classroom and in the school setting in general, and how for most I feel that society knows that they are the original men and they have to keep a conspiracy going in order to keep them out of the place they are supposed to be.

Ms. Harvey, mother of sons (17, 13), echoes Ms. Homes' statements in suggesting that society is not only against Black males, but that Black males are proactively targeted. We see in her statement how this issue links to self-esteem:

> Many challenges in the way that the society is made up to keep Black males down so to speak. They are targets and I think that White males are threatened by Black males more than any other group here. I think it's because we have been socializing into the White world, so to speak. We have some of the same values as they have and that's because our culture is somewhat changed by our history. The biggest challenge is to let them know that even though that is out there that can be overcome just by their own attitudes about themselves, what they expect from themselves, what they can pull out of themselves, and no matter what society dictates or tries to dictate.

Ms. Green says that whether as a byproduct of its oppressive dynamics or as a means of maintaining control, society emasculates Black males:

> "The biggest challenge I think my sons are faced with in this society is not being accepted in this society in any kind of way. Whether it be employment, educationally, socially, in any kind of way. In acceptance, just being accepted. I don't think Black men are accepted in this society. What I have done most is try to prepare my sons for the challenges that face them as Black men in a society that doesn't ac-

cept, see, or recognize Black men."

The mothers were aware of how Black males are confronted with debilitating stereotypes. For example, knowing how Black males are perceived in society, Mrs. Black refused to permit her son to wear an earring:

> One of the ways I can start looking back is in school. When you are bringing your children up and you know there might be certain things they want to do and you explain to them why they shouldn't do this because of color, knowing that being a Black child, especially a son, that you can't do, shouldn't do. I should say for a number of reasons—for your self, your moral self, growing up to get into the work place. I can give you an example. When Milton was in high school, it wasn't popular then at that time for guys to have earrings in their ear and he wanted to get one. A friend had pierced his ear and I made him cut it out for it to heal up. I explained to him that you're going to school, something happens, the first thing they'll do if you're around, you're Black, you have an earring in your ear and you'll be more likely to be singled out.

Similarly, Mrs. Miller did not allow her son to wear certain clothes. She was afraid that her son would become an indiscriminate victim of the police because of his skin color and sex.

I think that the police do pick out Black males more often than they do other ethnic groups to stop for example. There were a couple of incidents when my son was in col-

77

lege and even in high school when he was out looking for a job one day and he got stopped. It was just harassment. So to prepare him for that, first of all I let him know that this is a world that is not necessarily a just world. And secondly that if you wear your hair a certain way you could possibly be targeted and picked out even if you aren't doing something wrong. For example in Junior High, he wanted to be a break dancer, you know how they wore those jackets and they had those boom boxes that they carried? I didn't allow him to do that. He said, 'Mom, why can't I do that?' I said, 'Because you may just be running home from school one day because you're late and the police sees you with that jacket on like some of the other kids wear, and they may associate you with anything. I don't want them coming to my door saying that you were shot in the back or you were running from a scene of a crime because you had on a jacket like a thousand other Black kids.' So I tried to prevent him from that. I was really afraid. I was afraid as a mother with a son because of the gang influences and the society's reaction to Black males.

Mrs. Walton agrees with the other mothers; in addition, she connects those issues to self-esteem and self-concept:

People perceive young Black men by either what they experienced or what they heard, what they seen and they lump all Black men into that category. As far as my son is concerned, a lot of times he feels the repercussions of that stereotype and I do a lot of talking with him, to him, and a lot of encouragement to let him know that even though he doesn't fall into that category, don't let people put him into categories. That he is able to, just because a person thinks a certain way about an individual or about him doesn't necessarily mean that is true. . .

The following responses by working class mothers directly speaks to the dis-education of Black people (i.e., the process of schooling in the United States that renders many Blacks without the basic skills necessary to be successful in society). Their statements reflect their awareness of the ways in which society challenges the self-esteem and self-concept of Black males.

> **Mrs. Alison, mother of eight boys (20, 18, 12, 8, 6, 3, 2, 1).**
> They face society just not making them feel as if they're going to be something or somebody in the future. Just keeping them down, you know...I encourage them to go to school, be the best they can, get a good education. The challenges they face is to me society not wanting them to go to school, to make it in school if they don't because the teachers don't care if they learn, they just pass them on to the next grade.

> **Ms. Carr, mother of five sons (foster children, two of which she's had since birth) ages 17, 15, 11, 10, 8.**
> Leon and the rest of the Black boys have to face the economic problem in California. As a Black child,

he is not accepted in the White society. He has to do 4 or 5 times as much as the White child has to do. It's true. He has to excel 4 or 5 times over the rate expected of a White child. It's true. But they don't have the resources that the White children have. It's not their fault, it's society's fault. Consequently I think that the White society, especially California, I'm not talking about Eastern states, don't offer our Black children the necessities of life. They would rather our Black children go to public school with the concept of taking courses that aren't related to college or their future. I don't believe a Black child knowingly without parent's advice would sit and take electives subjects, don't take English, don't take math, don't take algebra, don't take world history, don't take science, don't take biology. These classes don't offer these children these things. They always want them to think they're going to be basketball players or mechanics or something like that, which is not good.

Ms. Carr believed that Black boys have to "do 4 or 5 times as much as the White child" to be successful in society. This appears to be a universal adage within Black communities. Ms. Waters' reflections represent Black mothers' typical response:

I told my children that in this community that you've got to work doubly hard. Twice as hard! Every day, Steven knew where we were living because we chose to live here. We moved here from L.A. and at that time he was in 1st grade and I said, 'I will not raise a child in L.A.' So we moved to Clearview [a predominately White affluent community] and so we moved here because my husband also was involved in almost what you are doing here now [referring to me]. He had attended Clearview Graduate School and when he moved here from L.A., of course going to the private graduate school, the people indicated where we would like to live, we knew nothing about this, of course we knew about Columbus [a neighboring less affluent city to Clearview] because my husband taught there but Clearview set up assistant housing and indicated that the school system was a very good school system. So we ended up here in Clearview. It started from 2nd grade, constantly every day. When he started at Rosehill School I remember three African American families at that school. Only three. I think that was a total of about nine kids at that whole school. So I had to instill in him when he was a little guy that he is going to have to work harder because he was a little different. When he was little I didn't really want to put that on him but we as African American people have got to work harder so it was instilled in him from 1st grade. Probably even before then I think but I thought that basically when we moved out here I started to instill in him that fact. It started in elementary school.

Even though she would have preferred to protect her son from such harsh realities, she knew she had to teach him at an early age to work twice as hard to get ahead in life. This is important to note because Mrs. Waters, a "nurturer," moved beyond her traditional feminine paradigm to equip her son to deal with the bitterness of life.

Mrs. Mills, mother of a son (16), and a daughter (18).
I tell John a lot that his biggest challenge is himself. Not thinking that he cannot be anything because of his skin. There are not any obstacles that you cannot reach. I always tell him to do his best. As a Black

man he has to be the best of the best and that is the true. He has to be not just as good but the best. That's true, he has to keep that in his mind. We all have to do that. You have to be the best of the best [she is referring to me]. You know, you go to school. You have to be the best in the classroom. And he knows he has to be the best of the best.

Some argue that the lack of appropriate Black male role models is problematic for Black communities, and the following two mothers agree:

Mrs. Peoples, mother of a son (15), and 2 daughters (9, 11).

Right now him seeing other male figures, knowing where his place is, how he is supposed to show himself. Right now it is a hard change for him going to a teenager and also to a young man and you see all these other young men and he's trying to figure, Where do I fit in? How am I supposed to represent myself? I am trying to keep him focused on the fact that everyone is an individual. You have a choice on who do you want to be and who do you want to be like. He doesn't have to be like everybody you see on the streets and carry yourself like that.

Ms. Jones says that her son's greatest challenge is "learning how to be male."

His biggest challenge as a male would be learning to be a male. He is around so many women. There's me and Daniesha at home, most of the time he has been with our family, there's all girls. Also

82

my sisters have girls, he tends to be around a lot of females. So just knowing what his manhood and his maleness should be. He's so quiet, that concerns me, so I try to get him involved in other activities and encourage him to spend more time with his father and grandfather so he can see some of the things they do.

In summary, the Black mothers in this study were aware of many pressing issues with respect to Black males. Most of these mothers interweave concerns about their sons' self-esteem and self-concept with the ubiquitous challenge of existing in an anti-Black and male society. They teach their sons that because of negative stereotypes and oppression, they will need to work twice as hard as their White counterparts in order to be successful. They discussed the lack of viable male role models to show them how to just be. Their awareness about Black male issues helps to prepare Black males negotiate, deal with, and overcome the challenging dynamics of Black manhood in the United States.

Mothers Define Masculinity and Manhood

Studies overwhelmingly suggest that Black males perceive themselves as not fitting the Western paradigm of masculinity (e.g., Hunter & Davis, 1992, 1994). Roberts (1994) concludes from his interviews that Black males are not comfortable with the socially defined traditional masculine ideal.

Little work has focused on how Black women concep-tualize, construct, and act upon their paradigm of manhood.

This is an important omission in the discourse of human development. As a majority of Black males are now being raised by single mothers and because Black mothers, single or married, play a significant role in raising their sons, it is necessary for scholars, social service providers, teachers, community members, and mothers themselves to understand how Black mothers define manhood. Understanding this dynamic could have far-reaching implications for educating, motivating, rehabilitating, getting along with, and empowering Black males.

Black women recognize the interrelationship of masculine and feminine experiences and expect Black males to contain in their sex-role identities a masculine and feminine self. Mrs. Mills offers these counter-traditional ideas of what it means to be a "real man":

Mrs. Mills: To be responsible, reliable, trustworthy, honest, a real man! I always told him he has to be just honest, responsible, be honorable. All that goes into being an honorable person. You have to be trustworthy and all that, so I tell him to be an honorable person. I think he will be because he says a lot of truths that surprises me sometime.

Interviewer: What does it mean to be a man?

Mrs. Mills: That is all those things that makes a man. *It makes a person too, a woman or anybody* [emphasis is mine].

Mothers were not directly asked to define manhood or masculinity unless they said something like what Mrs. Mills said ("a real man"). Then I probed by asking them to define what they meant. Table 5 is an alphabetical listing of terms used to express ideas of man, manhood, manliness, and masculinity that were extracted from the mothers' responses.

Table 5

Black Mothers' Alphabetical List of Manhood and Masculine Traits

A love of people
Believes that there is a God
Christian
Compassion for everyone
Concern for the human race
Financially independent
Good morals
Honest
Honorable
Married
Moral obligation
Reliable
Religious
Respect for others
Respects his elders

Respects his parents
Responsible
Responsible to his community
Strength
Strong character
Strong in mind and strong in heart
Treats other people the way he wants to be treated
Trustworthy
True to himself

When comparing the list in Table 5 with Eurocentric concepts of masculinity (e.g., aggression, ambition) and femininity (e.g., passive, illogical) listed in Table 2, I realize that these Black mothers have constructed a masculine model that is not Eurocentric. The qualities are balanced between the European and African models. For example, the Black mothers' list is composed of concepts such as being strong in mind and strong in heart, showing compassion for everyone, believing in a God, and being true to self. Ms. Evers' comments further illustrate this balance:

Ms. Evers: A few weeks ago Bobby was upset because some kids were beating him up or something and you have to be careful because you can't let other people beat you up but again you can't get so tough that you're beating up other kids. You have to be in the middle where you can defend yourself and you can also defend other people if they need it. And that was Manhood Lesson

Number One, Sharks and Guppies. Don't be either one! That was Manhood Lesson Number One. And later on he was crying about some little thing he bumped into, some way he hurt his foot. I never thought I would say this because I used to always get mad when other people did but I told him, 'You know what, you're going to be a man so you just can't be crying every time something happens to you. You are going to have to stop crying except on things that are really painful either physically or emotionally. If it really hurts, then cry because you need to. But every little thing, you're going to have cut that out.' That was Manhood Lesson Number Two. I was telling him one thing and my other son Carl heard me and he said this is a Manhood Lesson, I want to hear too. Oh OK! Then we got to Manhood Lesson Three. I can't remember at the moment but Carl said, 'You know, Mom, you should really write these down and make a book.' I said, 'OK!' That was funny because I was thinking of putting them on a scroll on the wall so we could keep up with them and I figured after a few I was going to forget what they were and then today Carl, no, one of them, said, 'I have a Manhood Lesson' they wanted to share with me. OK, so I think that is one thing that is catching on and I need to write these things down. When you interview Bobby, be sure to ask him. I think the Manhood Lessons make them feel good about being men. I'm trying to instill in them you are a man, a little one but you will be a bigger one soon.

Interviewer:	They haven't asked why they are learning these Manhood Lessons from a woman?
Ms. Evers:	Not yet. I think on the first one I explained to them even though I am not a man, I do know some things and as a man you are going to need to know this and since your dad is not here, I'm the one who has to teach you.

Later that day, when interviewing the twins, Carl and Bobby (8) and James (5) one son reiterated what the mother said:

Interviewer:	Can you tell me about guppies and sharks? What's a guppy?
Bobby:	A guppy is a small fish.
Interviewer:	What is a shark?
Bobby:	A real big man eating fish.
Interviewer:	What does your mom want you to be, a guppy or a shark?
Bobby:	Neither.
Interviewer:	Neither? Do you agree with that? Can you give me an example of being a shark?
Bobby:	It means to be kill people.

Interviewer:	What does it mean to be a guppy?
Bobby:	To be scared of them.
Interviewer:	So you want to be somewhere in the middle. Can you tell me an example of being somewhere in the middle?
Bobby:	Don't hit people but only in defense.
Interviewer:	In what?
Bobby:	In defense!
Interviewer:	Oh in defense, OK.

In desiring to become a man, Bobby is seeking a middle point between a shark (traditional masculinity) and a guppy (traditional femininity). His mother is helping him to achieve a balance between toughness and being a "cry baby." Also, in Ms. Evers' "Manhood Lessons" we gain insight into how Black mothers define manhood and masculinity.

In the following comments, being honorable emerges as a key ingredient in Black mothers' definition of manhood. Honor becomes an umbrella term for other concepts such as honesty and trustworthiness:

| Mrs. Price: | Honesty, being honest. Respectful. Concern for the human race. Honesty, concern for everybody. Respectful and responsible. |

Mrs. Walton:	Honesty, feel that he has self-worth, a lot of things! Strength.
Ms. Jones:	Qualities? Responsible, to be self-sufficient, to be able to take care of himself and have a love for people and be truthful.

In the comment below, Ms. Evers never mentions the word honorable, but it is implied when she says "having a strong character." She wants her son to be honorable with respect to children he may have in the future, to other people in general, and to themselves. However, she especially expects her sons to be honorable in their relationships with women:

Ms. Evers:	I think they should have a strong character.
Interviewer:	What's a strong character?
Ms. Evers:	I'll give you a couple of things. One is how they treat women. Obviously that will be important. I have had experiences that I didn't like and I don't want to turn out sons that will do the same thing. But of course I can do anything I want to and they will be who they—they will make choices that I have no influence over, but I want them to be at least self-supporting. I don't want them to be living off of somebody else,

90

and I want them to be honest in their dealings with people. If they feel they are in a situation, like with a woman or whatever, that is not right for them, instead of staying there and dipping here and there that they just get out. I want them to hopefully be married. Have their family and stay there. In the event if that doesn't happen, I want them to be responsible for children that they make. I want them in their character to be honest in their dealings with other people but also within themselves.

Judging by the number of times it was mentioned and how it was often isolated as a single quality, it is clear that being responsible takes primacy over the other characteristics that define manhood. Some mothers like Ms. Harvey simply said, "Responsibility. That's number one for me." Other mothers kept their responses brief and to the point but added a definition. For example, Mrs. White said, "Responsibility, really responsible people. Be able to take care of themselves and whoever they get involved with. Just be able to handle their own affairs, I guess." Being responsible in this context goes beyond the individual and his immediate family and is tied to a community. Ms. Jackson, mother of one son (24) acknowledges this aspect of manhood:

91

I think responsibility, responsibility. Responsible to himself. Truth of himself and that he is also responsible to his community and beyond that I don't know if I care about a whole lot else. If he could just be that and do that, I know that covers a lot and it does for him, then I am OK with that.

According to the mothers in this study, being respectful starts with one's self and extends to one's family and other relationships. Three mothers comment on being respectful as a key component of manhood:

Mrs. Black: Especially for young men it is important to have some kind of respect for yourself and others and they have got ten good respect for not being disrespectful within our family. When they grew up I tried to instill in them to work, to take care of themselves, don't do anything out there to bring shame back on us. No matter if you're out there having fun, and you're doing all your things I still say that it's not only you, it's your whole family out there and if anything goes wrong, it comes back. I think I wanted them to have respect, some kind of moral obligation, respect for others.

Mrs. Walton: Show respect and think about the woman in their lives as treating them with the same respect that they would treat their mother or sister. I always taught them to treat other people the way they want to be treated.

Mrs. Peoples:	Respect for people, how he carries himself, I think is very important because that opens a lot of doors for you.

These Black mothers hold spirituality as an important dimension of masculinity. Most mothers connect spirituality with church, "God," and the Bible:

Mrs. Alison:	Moral, good morals and that's why I take them to church. I try to teach them at home to be good men, do good things.
Ms. Carr:	Religious beliefs that there is a God, he has to do what is written in the Bible, more or less. He has to learn to respect his elders, he has to learn to how to respect his parents.

The following mother believes that being Christian is a key aspect of manhood. She also comments that connecting the strength of one's mind to the heart is important.

Mrs. East, mother of two sons (12, 2) and one daughter (9).
First and foremost is compassion of everyone. Other than that I would like to see him carry himself as a Christian and you know what falls under that. Just be a good person all around. I want him to be a strong man but have a sense of being a man, not that image that you get on the streets. Not that. I would like for him to have street smarts but not the point where they

say, "He's bad." I don't want that for my son. I want him to be strong in his mind and strong in his heart.

Embedded in some of the mothers' comments is the notion of being self-sufficient and independent. This may appear to be linked to the Eurocentric masculine value of rugged individualism, but it is not. In the mothers' view, an adult should not be dependent on his/her family for food, clothes, and shelter, but should be able to contribute to his/her family by working in and outside of the home. Income should go to benefiting the collective rather than the individual. Mrs. Myers, mother of a son (36) and two daughters (35, 31) says, "The thing I wanted most was for my children to be independent financially."

In conclusion, the mothers desire a type of manhood for their sons that strikes a balance between traditional masculinity and femininity. This section has laid the foundation for the argument that Black mothers are well prepared on many levels to raise their sons to become men. Effective Black mothers possess a variety of personal characteristics that help them raise their sons. They are acutely aware of challenges that are specific to Black men. The goals for their sons' manhood are arguably healthier than the traditional model.

Methods Black Mothers Employ to Raise Their Sons

How do Black mothers put their personal characteristics, awareness, and African-centered tenets into practice?

Black mothers use themselves as models. They point out examples, set expectations, seek to expose, use their words as transforming mechanisms, and create sacred space and time for talking. We will explore parenting styles using these teaching methods. Formerly homeless, separated from her husband, and ill, Mrs. East uses herself as an example. She believes that this is an effective method of showing her children adulthood behavior:

> Even though I'm home, they never seen me at home other than when I was sick. I would volunteer at the schools, I would volunteer at the churches, I would go to school. Now that I am at home, I'm going to start my own business. I let them know I am doing this. I read a lot around them, I encourage them to read, things like that. I work with them, when they are doing their homework I work with them on it. If they have a problem and I know they are supposed to know it, I still work with them on it. I let them know, with me I'm doing something, I'm not just sitting doing nothing. I'm always doing something to try to better myself and to make a better life for them. When I was going to school, he was like, 'Mom, why are you going to school?' Because I would get home and I would just ache all over, and I said, 'Because I want to make a better life for us. I want things to be better.' When I wasn't going to school anymore, I let them know when I started to order my classes in the mail and also the different things that I'm doing to start my business and stuff like that, I talk to them about it so they know that's what life is all about.

Similarly, Mrs. Miller used herself as a teaching tool as she modeled the behavior that she wanted her son to manifest:

> Just living what I preached. One of the things that I always felt troubled about with parents and children is we have these double standards. 'Don't do as I do, do what I say to.' I tried very hard but I'm not a perfect parent and I wasn't a perfect parent but I tried very hard to live out those things that I expected him to do and to become. I didn't drop him off at church, I went to church with him. I took him to church. When it came to dress, I didn't dress like a skeezer, I tried to dress appropriately so he would have some examples of what it looked like to be a person going to work and doing what they needed to do in the work force. The attitudes that I wanted him to model are the attitudes that I feel I exhibited to be able to be a well-rounded person. To be able to say I'm sorry if I made a mistake.

Ms. Carr uses the media to assist her in developing manhood:

> I have tried to get them off TV so much because it's not good. A lot of times I just turn the TV off and let them read a lot. I buy a lot of Black magazines so they can see Black role models, so they can sit down and read them, so they can know some positive reinforcement. Not all Black men are doomed. I buy a lot of books and magazines that have Black businessmen in it, a lot of time black newsmen come on TV, I said, 'There's a nice newsman.

Mrs. Black used negative images from the community to teach her son:

> When he was out of high school, he really didn't like school so we went for a drive in the car. I didn't drive then so he took me and we just drove around Columbus and I pointed out guys standing on the street, doing nothing, been out of school, just hanging around and I was telling him, 'This is what I don't want you to do.' He'll tell you things like when they were growing up, I wouldn't allow them as young men to sit in front of the house. If they came up with beer, they could not do it in front of the house, they knew not to stop here. The most memorable is taking him for a ride after high school to tell him what I expected of him now that he was out of school.

Many of the mothers said that they establish a set of expectations as a means of guiding their sons. Mrs. Black says, "I always try to tell them the things that we would not accept. Some parents might allow those things [earrings] but they were just not acceptable and they understood that." In this same manner Ms. Evers uses her expectation as a vision of where she wants her sons to be or, more precisely, not to be:

> I don't know that so much I have a clear vision of what's ahead because I'm not the best at planning ahead but at the same time I have certain goals and even though I zigzag on my way to them I do get there. So I think by thinking, OK, I'm not going to have some crazy little boys that are helpless, I'm not

going to have that. I may not know exactly how to make sure that happens, or I will read, or I will try, or I will watch or I will ask and I think a lot of it is instinct too. 'No, you're not going to be that kind of person and I'm going to make sure that you're not.'

Mrs. Alison says:

Sometimes I asked them questions on what they want to be. I used to, I don't do this no more, I should start it back up. I used to have Dennis and Jamal say, 'I want to be a doctor,' and I just make them repeat it over and over. [Laughter] I should make them do it again. I asked John John one day, 'What do you want to be when you grow up?' He was only about 5 or 6 at the time and he said, 'A strawberry picker.' And I was like, 'Why?' He said, 'Because I love strawberries, they taste good.' Trying not to put him down, I said, 'Well, if you going to be a strawberry picker, why don't you grow your own strawberries, then you can pick your own strawberries. Be a picker but have your own strawberries, don't pick for nobody else. Pick for yourself.' He was like, 'OK.' I was like, 'Oh man, a strawberry picker!'

Some Black mothers use exposure and travel as method of instruction. Clearly economics might determine the extent to which travel is possible. Mrs. Walton made sure to expose her sons to the world beyond their backyard in South Central Los Angeles. Dr. Washington's mother was single while he was growing up, yet, his mother was the impetus for eventual exposure to the world. She loved to travel. First, Mrs. Walton's comments and then, Dr. Washington's:

> *Mrs. Walton:* I remember when my kids were growing up I always exposed them to a lot of different things and different types of people. Going places, family type outings, camping trips, restaurants, teaching them how to eat in restaurants, behavior in restaurants, going on camping trips where they had to interact with other people putting up tents, boy scouts, etc. Exposure to different people, different cultures, growing up and raising kids in South Central, there wasn't always a lot of that but I have always been real active in other activities and taking them on picnics and other group settings where there were a lot of different people around. Always trying to point out good things that people are doing and showing them negative things. All of that plays a part in pulling things together.

Dr. Washington (51) son of Mrs. Philips.

We were taken to Detroit and from there we went to Canada at 12 years of age and I was excited. I was seeing a new culture and eating new foods while living in Canada. And her dream was for me to have many experiences—she enjoyed traveling. So through her eyes, I got the traveling bug. Being encouraged by her, like I said, at age of 5 and then 12 getting involved with the Hi-Y I traveled to several areas within the state of Mississippi. At 13 I got involved in the civil rights movement, which then took me into

Washington, DC, at a very formative point of my life. From there I went to other states, but that was due to her encouragement, her permission, her interest in the civil rights movement. I was also very fortunate to visit and live in Africa three times.

In the beginning of this chapter I quote Genesis 1:1–3 in which God used His/Her voice to bring light into the world. With the power of their voices, Black mothers may move and transform their sons. Donald (29) explains how his mother's (Mrs. Miller) words changed his life, moving him from a spiritually dead lifestyle to one that now reflects his spiritual enlightenment.

I was in the 11th grade and I was a really serious player. A lot of guys say they're players in high school but I was on a string. I was on the phone with a girl, me and my mom were close, well she taught me how to make prank calls, we were close in every way! I'm on the phone with this girl and she's telling me how much she loves me, wait a minute, I click over and another girl is on the line and she's telling me. I put them on hold and tell my mother to pick up the other phone. She picks up the phone and I got this girl telling me how much she loves me, if she could she'd have my baby and all this junk. So I click over and let her hear the other girl. And she's doing the same drama and then I told them all, 'I'll call ya'll back,' I got off the phone.

My mother came in the room and said, 'I didn't raise you to be like that,' and she said it not in a condescending way, kind of like the same way my grandfather said [referring to an incident that occurred in his youth with his grandfather]—it pierced me. 'I didn't raise you to be like that.' 'I'm looking at you and see the way you're headed.' I say, 'What are you talking about?' 'You don't have a job, you have all these women, and you don't respect any of them.' She said, 'You know who you are?' I said, 'No.' She said, 'You're your father.'

I didn't know him, I spent a total of two weeks time with him and I didn't like him. I never really dealt with him, I sort of moved that away to the side. When she said that, it broke me. I never been around him, how am I being like him? She said, 'You're being just like him.' And I think that very next week, I went and got a job and kept a job from the 11th grade on, never been jobless. I still dealt with the woman thing because you know how we are. Some of us at least as we grow and we discover the things of the world but *those words changed my life* [emphasis is mine].

When I came to grips with the fact that God had designed me to be a different man than what I was being, *it was those words that rang in my heart* [emphasis is mine]. 'I didn't raise you to be like that,' but a man of integrity. When she said those things, it shook me up as a teenager. It shook me up, that's kind of deep.

Later on in life, I was able to take those things that she said and really apply them and make some changes in my life. Stop being a player, stop dogging women out, keep a job and stop lying to the women and all that. I was most fascinated with women that told me they loved me more than anything else. That was probably one of the most powerful things that ever happened in terms of what she said or did to me that influenced the outcome of my life. As I look back now, I was destined and I know more of my father now, I was destined to be just like him and that was a scary thought. I was 7 out of 11 kids and knows them all by name but just like my father, that's how I could have been like that if I didn't have a mother like that and not be in and God not watching over me and I would have been just like that. I saw women as a trophy and a prize and all that so what else are they supposed to do but be there for when I want that kind of thing. I was thankful, I think about that often actually, what she said. I share that with friends of mine who still struggle in the area of being a man of integrity.

All mothers used dialogue to teach, guide, and develop their sons into men. Many of these mothers mentioned that they had a special place in which to talk to their sons. Ms. Jackson said she would call her son up on her bed when she wanted to engage him about the challenges of life. She firmly believes that those sacred interactions ultimately shaped the productive adult life of her son. Beginning with Ms. Harper, mother of a son (13), four mothers comment on their special times and space for dialogue.

Interviewer: When you are laying on the bed is that a good time for you?

Ms. Harper: He might tell me what's really going on with him, his frustrations and when he lays next to me I know he wants to talk. It has always been like that. When I'm laying on the couch or on the floor, on the bed it doesn't matter. He'll come to me. I'll be like he wants to say something. I'll wait. I'll say anything on your mind? Sometimes he doesn't want anything, he just want to lay next to me. All right! If he really wants to, it's that look. That's what he doesn't understand about the look. I say, 'You want to tell me something?' 'No.' 'Yes you do.' 'How do you know?' 'It's just a look that you give me and I just know the look.' And we might talk about School, his friends, what's so frustrating, what made him so mad.

Mrs. Eve, mother of 3 sons, 40, 34 (1 died at 26), and two daughters (42, 38).

Interviewer: How often did you have these sessions?

Mrs. Eve: At least twice a month and sometimes, as often as they felt they needed it.

Interviewer: They'd come to you and say?

Mrs. Eve: It's time for council. Let's meet. A family meeting. That included all six of my children, at that time I had six and myself. And this is what we would sit down and do.

103

Mrs. Piper, mother of one son (15).

Mrs. Piper: I tried to be straight with them and teach them good values. I don't sugar coat things, I talk to them harsh because reality is harsh sometimes and I know how their friends are out there talking. I have to talk so they understand that life is not easy if you don't have an education, money, good values. I try to talk to him often. Seems like a lot of times he likes to talk late at night.

Interviewer: Does he just start talking?

Mrs. Piper: Uh, huh. He just opens up so I don't say nothing, I just let him talk. I think when my daughters are asleep, he's free, where they don't get involved because usually they're nosy and they interrupt and he's like, he doesn't want to talk.

Mrs. Green: If something was a visual, if we saw something or an incident or something we saw riding in the car, or sitting out somewhere eating or shopping or whatever the case was or even a scenario on the news, we talk about it. I believe you must have meals together because that's probably the real time you have together once they grow up to a certain age. That is the time most we spent talking. Generally something would come up, something would occur during their days or a scenario of something we have seen. Always, my children even today, Damien at 20, they don't go to bed without sharing in the evening. Even when they went out, when they go out and come in, they sit down on my bed and we talk about the experience that they had what they saw. I tell them what functions, what will work there for them. What will function for them.

We discovered in this section that Black mothers use diverse methods to teach their sons. Timely words coupled with ongoing dialogue were most often used. Black mothers often use themselves as examples to imbue their sons with respect, a sense of responsibility, compassion, individual strength that benefits the collective, and honesty which is tantamount, in this respect, to manhood, adulthood, or just being human.

Life's Lessons: Sexuality, Survival, and Responsibility

In the first part of this section, not only will we examine life lessons taught by Black mothers to their sons, but we will also analyze topics such as sexuality, respect, and knowing one's self. In the second part of this section, I will look at the literature in light of some of the findings of this project. Lastly, we will close by presenting various dynamics and components of Black mother-son interactions that will help us gain additional insight into this relationship.

In a society such as the United States in which White cultural chauvinism, hegemony, and supremacy are constant (Bush, 1995), Black children may struggle with their identities (Duncan, 1994). For Black parents the challenge goes beyond teaching children to like themselves. Some Black parents struggle so that their children do not hate themselves and others who look like them. Mrs. Waters talked a lot about growing up in a predominately White, affluent city, which led to symptoms of Black self-hate early in her son's life.

When he came home, if we had African American company, he would walk through real fast. He was about 8 or 9. But if we had European company he would say 'Hi, how are you?' So I had taught my kids that they are the love of my life, but I guess it was time to teach them that they are not loved by everybody. But I remembered after a few times that it bothered me because my kids should know better. I remember getting him and sitting him down and talking with him and that's when I really had to focus in on who he really was. I sat down with him and said 'Look, I have noticed you not being receptive to African American company as you are to Europeans.' I knew I had not done this before so I knew it was time. I said, 'You are showing favoritism towards these people,' and I said, 'You have to act like who you are and what we are.' And I scratched his little arms and I said, 'You see what you are. You are a Black man.'

Mrs. Waters said similar events occurred during that time; for example, he tried to avoid her in public. Mrs. Waters believes that by confronting her son about being Black and male at an early age, he began to like

106

and appreciate himself. She says that today her son is married to a "beautiful dark skinned woman."

It is often stated that one of the problems with young people is that they have lost respect for their elders. Many of the mothers recall a time when children said, "yes sir" or "ma'am" to every adult. Being respectful is very important to Ms. Harvey. Here she gives her son a valuable lesson concerning being respectful:

> I say it, I demonstrate, I don't care, if anything comes up, even with their own friends, I will point out things that are appropriate or anything like that. With friends I tell them, if I see someone—like my oldest had a friend. When I first met him, I wasn't too sure about him, his attitude, the way he presented himself when he first came into the house. You don't come into anyone's house and not speak to their parents or anyone. I didn't like that so I told him, 'I did not like that. No one walks in here and not speak to your mother or anyone else. You say hello.' I said, 'He walked right past me.' He said, 'He is not like that.' I said, 'I don't know, you better speak to him because next time he comes in I will speak to him about it.' Any opportunity you have like that, you say, 'speak to this friend,' 'choose your friends wisely.' When I come in I am going to speak to your mother or anyone. You shake hands. He said, 'He is not like that.' 'Well you better speak to him.' So the next time he came in, he was a little better. [Laugh] He spoke up. I loved that. I am like that. That is respect to me. I don't let anybody, any of his friends, or anyone else come in and not show respect to me. I figure if his friends walk in and not show respect, what that shows of him, about his friends, choosing of his friends and everything? And also vice versa. When he goes into other people's houses and he sees

107

a grandmother or anybody he never walks in and not say, 'Hello, how are you doing?' He has to give his grandmother a kiss and hug every time he sees her. That is just showing respect for other people. It's showing that he is a gentleman—a man with certain amount of dignity I should say.

On the surface, Ms. Harvey taught her son about respect, especially for elders. On a deeper level, this was a lesson in protocol or culture, which prescribes how children and adults interact and defines appropriate adult Black male behavior. In this cultural context, an adult Black male who respects his elders is a man with dignity.

The mothers taught their sons to have compassion for the less fortunate. When Dr. Washington was a child, his mother took in physically challenged elderly women. Just watching his mother's benevolent actions could have been enough to teach him about being compassionate. However, Dr. Washington was an active participant in the care of these women:

> My mother brought in an elderly lady when I was around 11 who was blind, stroke ridden, and totally confined to bed. She stayed in my grandmother's bedroom. We assisted in the bathing of her, combing her hair, making sure she had cold water. Water is very important because it is very hot in the South. And what I learned from that is that you may have health one day, but it could be gone tomorrow. The reason why you can see the Creator is real. [pause] It is about helping somebody who really needs the help. I learned through my mother and grandmother caring

for this lady that it did not bother them that they could not get her daughters to come to visit her. Through that I learned you don't put conditions on your love because another relative is acting up, you can't challenge the situation. I learned through that to appreciate my health, to cherish my health and to watch what I put into my body. I feel that through them caring for this lady, they had two senior citizens that they kept in the house for many years. I could get them to take their medicine when no one else could, so I felt I relate very comfortably with senior citizens. Those invaluable lessons I learned just by them bringing those two people into my life and I will always cherish that. When I was having difficulties in undergraduate school and being harassed by some of my White classmates, my mother would say, 'Think about Milly if you think you have it bad.' That would make me smile and have the strength to go back out and challenge the situation.

Through watching and participating in acts of compassion, Dr. Washington, who currently spends time volunteering at a nursing home, was able to extract other lessons that were facilitated by his mother. Appreciating what he had in life and using the knowledge of his "blessings" to motivate himself, eating right, and learning how to love his family unconditionally were also priceless lessons that he learned from this experience with his mother. Mrs. Price underscores this in a second example of how Black mothers teach their sons compassion:

When Tracy was about—this Christmas it will be about 3 years ago so Tracy was 5 almost 6. Tracy gets all these toys and clothes and books and stuff for Christmas and for his birthday and Kennon has little brother and another little sister that are older. And Ms. Wright has boys, they're not as fortunate as we are. Tracy got all this stuff and I told him how he should give some of the things his brothers had given him and his aunt and cousins. I told him to wrap them back up and give them to Kennon's little brother and sister and Catherine's little boys. I wanted to teach him that to me it was a sin to have too much and there are other kids out there that may need something even though they are just material things. I wanted him to see and understand about giving. That really sticks out in my mind and he was just proud of himself that he did that.

In this next excerpt Mrs. Mills gives her son a lesson that centers on being honorable, but like so many other examples we find that more than one principle or quality of manhood is being taught:

> The products are the children, they show how good a person you are. I try to show him examples of people that I know as they come up. 'Look what this person is doing, look where he started from, but look what he has done. How he supports his children.' Not just celebrities but people you know. Just regular people that you know that have worked hard. I know this one guy, he is not an educated person, he works hard in his job, he's not educated, but on the weekends, he'll go pick up junk and recycle it. Cardboard and stuff. That is honorable. He is doing what he can do best for his family. He knows his job is not meeting the needs, and he takes his responsibility to do it.

110

I pointed it out to him that it doesn't matter about degrees. It matters what you do with the best of what you have and make the best of it and he does that. You can see him around picking up the stuff. He is a very humble person, education doesn't matter. He is trying his best. That is what it takes. Doing the best you can. He is an older man so he is doing what he knows. I try to take examples when I see it. If you point out people in their everyday that they can see what they are doing. It may not be all fantastic to someone else's eyes but it is to me because he is being the best man he can be with his family.

Perhaps the most significant lesson being taught here is that Mrs. Mills roots a man's value, worth, or character in the outcome of his children. Other lessons include the value of hard and honest work and being humble and responsible.

For these next two sons, learning to apologize as children would prove to be advantageous in their current relationships with women. They both believe that they are better men because they learned how to apologize from their mothers.

Dr. Washington: Learning to apologize when I am at odds with another person, including my wife, will make me who I am.

Interviewer: Did she apologize to you?

Dr. Washington: Oh yes, my mother could do that with no problem. As a result what I share with my wife, I have been married to her for over 13 years, if I offend her I could apologize to her publicly in front of a thousand people because I can do the same thing with my sister.

Donald: Now even in relationships with other people or women or friends I am willing to apologize. I learned that from her because sometimes she would do some crazy stuff every now and then. For the most part she was like this, now and then she would go like that. She would come back and say, 'I'm sorry, I apologize.' The first time she did that, it blew me away. I never heard a parent apologize to any child. That's all right with me—I respect that! OK! So every now and then when we would get into it, I would look for when I knew she was wrong, I'd look for an apology. Sometimes I would get it and sometimes I wouldn't. She taught me how to be real in the sense that even when you're involved in something and you think you're right, but it's important to re-analyze it and see if you were right and even if you were, how you affect the other person. I've learned there's more than one reason why you have to apologize for certain situations.

Below, the lessons Mrs. East taught her 12-year-old son concerning honesty gets put to a test. She contends that what her son knows about being honest is directly derived from her teachings:

> He had an incident at school where they went into the cafeteria and he took an ice cream and he was with a friend. When they came out of the cafeteria, he threw it; so the person that caught them didn't see what he did. They just asked him, 'What were you doing in the cafeteria?' And he said he went in there to get an ice cream and so they suspended him for suspicion of stealing so I said, 'Why did you tell that when they didn't see you?' He said, 'because I didn't want to get myself in worse trouble.' He said, 'That is what I went in there for,' and so he was supposed to go to camp. And he said, 'If they tell me I can't go to camp, then that's the consequences I have to suffer because I know what I did was wrong.' Right there, that let me know he started to mature...It wasn't the way I handled it but the way he handled it and the concepts that I taught him, because it could never come from his dad, what his dad has taught him, so I know it had to come from what I taught him.

When discussing this project with both male and female friends and colleagues, or hearing related issues being debated on the radio, common concerns are: "Who is going to teach Black boys about sex?" and, "Who is going to teach them how to survive if there is no father around?" At this point we will exclude the role of extended families and examine what Black mothers are teaching their sons about sexuality and survival.

The degree of comfort varied for both mothers and sons as they engaged in conversations about sex. For some sons, it was easy talking to their mothers concerning these matters while their mothers found it difficult. On the other hand, some sons found it difficult to talk to their mothers, while the mothers found it rather routine. What was difficult to untangle were the reasons for the discomfort. For sons, was it due to having to talk to a woman or just general difficulties some children have in talking about sex with an adult, especially a parent? For mothers who experienced discomfort, what thoughts, feelings, memories, and unresolved issues about sex were raised?

In this first excerpt, both mother and son are uncomfortable. Ms. Harvey always thought it was the "father's role" to discuss sex. However, this belief does not stop her from aggressively addressing premature sexual experiences:

> When he first went to middle school, when he was in 6th grade, I thought, he is going to middle school, oh the hormones are—I needed to talk to him. I called him downstairs. I was sitting there and he walked in, and said 'Mom, I hate when you do this.' I was sitting on the edge of the couch, he knew something was up. There was a little girl around the corner, she was in high school. 'Martin, what in the world are you thinking? A girl in high school going out with some little boy in middle school. You need to stop this, I'm not going to have you going around there and she's not coming around here.' You know how they say, 'Let this go,' but I could not let this go. I don't think so! 'You are in middle school, 6th, 7th, 8th grade, she is high school. She shouldn't be around here in the first place. You can't go there, she can't come here. There are so many diseases.' He said, 'I

114

know, Mama.' It was like he didn't want me to talk. 'You don't think I am not going to talk to you about that?' I thought I shouldn't have to do that, that is what the father is to do. And I said, 'Well, I don't exactly think that is right, but I am your mother and I am going to talk to you about anything I want to talk to you about.'

Two themes that many Black mothers reiterated were (1) abstinence and the need for sons to be aggressive in terms of protecting themselves from diseases and (2) preventing unwanted pregnancies. Mrs. Alison preaches abstinence to her sons, but she realizes that she cannot control everything that they do:

I tell them, 'You guys shouldn't have sex before you get married, you should just wait till you get married. The most beautiful thing in the world is when a man and woman can marry each other and both of them be virgins. There's nothing with being a virgin. You don't have to be out there doing what everybody else do. Save yourself.' And I talk to them like that but then you can talk to your kids but they're still going to do what they going to do.

I found out that Kanard, he was about 15 years old, he had a little girlfriend, and he took a shower with her one day at our house with all his brothers at home. He got it for that. He didn't get a whuppin', he just got a stern talking to and he never did it again. So Todd calls himself pulling the same thing. We told Todd, 'You don't do that crap in here and disrespect me, you disrespect Joe, you

115

disrespect all your brothers and you disrespect this house and the girl. Look at all this disrespect you throwing around.' He didn't seem like he was, it was going in one ear and coming out the other. He kept doing it. Every time me and Joe would leave the kids home alone, this school girl would come over and they would just get busy, whenever they felt like it. They'd locked the kids out the bedroom and stuff and so we went way off on him, took his door off, just made it miserable for him.

So he got mad and he moved out. That was one time he moved with my mom because he just didn't want nobody telling him he couldn't have sex. 'So we don't want you to go, but if you feel that strongly, you gotta leave, I wish you wouldn't go but if that's the way you feel.' I tried to stop him but he went on but he came back through. When he came back, he had time to think and he knew he was wrong, and he said he was wrong and he asked to come back, but I tell him, 'Don't ever trust a girl if she tells you she's on birth control because even if she is on birth control she might have a disease and you go and have sex with her and she gives you a disease and then you won't be able to have no kids or you'll be sick the rest of your life. You can get AIDS and die so always wear a rubber.' I give him rubbers all the time, I don't know if he's using them or playing with them or what but since I know he has done it and acting like he couldn't stop, now I have to approach it that way, I don't like it, but what can I do? Help trying to prevent a baby and he knows he don't want no kids, he knows he can't afford no kids and he knows he don't want no diseases so I'll go and buy him some, I keep rubbers often.

Ms. Green also feels that it is the father's role to teach sons about sex, and was uneasy about talking to her sons about it. Much of her discomfort was centered on her belief that it was certain things she could not tell her son about sex because she could only experience it as a woman whereas a man could, in her opinion, paint a more vivid picture for boys to understand.

Ms. Green: With both of my kids, when it came down to different points, different things in life and they were usually sexual, those were very difficult times for me because I couldn't tell them things, you know. I could tell them from a political standpoint, that's very true but I couldn't say—I remember with Mike in particular, he said, 'Mom, I wonder what it's really like, what it really seems like.' And I said, 'I don't know about this'—what could I tell him? [Much laughter] The first time we talked about sex and him wanting to explore and everything I said, 'Oh my God what am I going to do?' I really didn't know what to do but what I did was I went to the drugstore and bought a box of Trojans and I put them on his dresser. He came to me, my sons will come to me about anything, he came to me and he went, 'How do I do them? How do I use them?' How do I tell him how to use them? I don't have this experience. This was probably one of the most hysterical moments I think I can remember, mostly with

117

	Mike. I remember we laid back on my bed, I read the direction to him, we read the directions together. I asked him if he had anymore questions. He said, 'No.' I said, 'OK, fine.'
Interviewer:	How would it have been different with a man?
Ms. Green:	A man probably would have just told him!
Interviewer:	A man would have just told him, and that would have been better?
Ms. Green:	Yeah!
Interviewer:	Maybe a man wouldn't have taken the time to read the directions, and maybe he wouldn't have told him you shouldn't pull it down tight all the way. You as his mother took the time and read it to him. It was uncomfortable for you, but how did he leave that experience lacking because he didn't come to a man?
Ms. Green:	I don't know, maybe—
Interviewer:	I really can't express, 'What it feels like.'

I asked Ms. Green's son Mike (27) what it was like to learn about sex from his mother. He said that talking about sex with his mother made him feel uncomfortable and that there were some issues that he would have pre-ferred talking to a man about. Yet, even with that uneasy feeling, Mike and his mother did talk. Below Mike shares the consequences of these conversations:

Interviewer:	Do you feel that you lost something because you learned a lot of what you know about sex from your mother?
Mike:	My mother helped me with the emotional and feeling aspect of sex. I don't know if a man would have taught me about all that stuff. I think I was better off talking to a woman. Do you know what I mean?
Interviewer:	Yes.

We will explore more dialogue with mothers and sons in the next chapter. However, it is clear from this example, and others, that Black mothers take an active role in teaching their sons about sexuality, which, in this age of sexually transmitted diseases, might be a lesson in learning literally how to survive.

To recap, the mothers' survival lessons can be thought of as having a son learn "how to stand on his own two feet." This can be a difficult lesson for Black mothers to teach their sons. According to King and Mitchell (1990, 1991), Black mothers are often caught between the proverbial rock and hard place: either they overprotect their sons from an oppressive society or they allow them to be overexposed to the harshness of an anti-Black and male world. I bring this issue up in the group interview with new mothers of sons. Mrs. Ross, mother of a 1-month-old son, responds:

119

Interviewer:	Sometimes people say that a strong Black mother can be a negative influence on her sons because she will go to bat too much for her son and he will not learn how to be a man. Is that a concern of yours?
Mrs. Ross:	Yes, my husband and I have talked about it. In his opinion, he is taking the Scripture, when a man and a woman become joined together, the man leaves his parents and cleaves to his wife. He believes a man shouldn't leave home until he's ready to go and get married. I believe different. I believe that women, so to speak, kind of mess up their sons when they do that. I believe after he reaches the age of manhood, I believe he should either be in school, or he should be in the service if that is what it's going to be or he should be out on a job. He shouldn't be home, waiting to find his wife and then move out. I think it ruins them, it lets them know that it's OK to be home under Mom, it's no pressure going out getting a job, and even if you do have a job it shows them it doesn't give them a sense of responsibility. They need to be out before they find their wife, they need to be out learning how to pay bills, learning how to accept responsibility for their actions and that won't happen to my son. I will still teach him he needs to know responsibility.

Both mother and father are present in the home, and it is the mother who assumes the "masculine" position that her son should be exposed to the world while the father wants to protect his son from such dynamics, i.e., the "feminine" position. In this next excerpt, Mrs. Myers is torn between allowing her son to stand on his own feet and intervening on her son's behalf with a situation that involves her son and his father.

Mrs. Myers: I can remember there was a painful experience when he was thirteen, I do remember this. We were out in the backyard and for some reason his father got upset with him and he did strike him at the time. I remember that. That upset me so because I was out there but I didn't say anything. I just went in the house. I'm glad I did it that way. That wasn't a situation that I should have interfered with, but it was so shocking to me that his father got so upset with him that he hit him. Just a one time kind of thing, I don't even remember what the discussion was but I decided not to get involved. Then I had some serious feelings about it; did he feel I was deserting him or whatever? You think about it later, that's his father, so I knew he loved him and I did the right thing, got out of the situation before I did something.

Interviewer: Did that feeling of desertion creep up in other areas?

Mrs. Myers: It might have given him the idea, 'I gotta look out for myself. My mother is not always going to be there for me.'

121

Ms. Jones is teaching her son how to stand on his own and be responsible. In this particular situation she lets him deal with the consequences of his actions and uses it as a teaching tool:

> He has learned this one now, I told him, 'Try not to count on anyone except for yourself. Someone else comes through, consider it a blessing.' He tends to slack at homework and at his junior high school. They have to do study hall, which means they miss the bus. He tried to set up an appointment where Donna would pick him up. She didn't come through, so he had to walk and that's an hour walk home but if he had did his homework and turned it in, he would have never had to miss the bus. She said she would do it, she came late but I try to let him know that it was a blessing that she was going to come for him, but don't make this a habit because people won't always come through. If you do what you have to do then you don't have to worry about all those other things. It was out of her way too.

Interaction with police can be a survival issue. Police brutality involving Black males and White police officers is still all too common (Mauer, 1994). Earlier, we discovered that Mrs. Miller did not want her son to wear certain clothes for fear he would be singled out by the police and become a victim of senseless police brutality. Along these same lines, Mrs. Mills gives her son a survival lesson:

> I'm always talking. 'Don't run home like that.' Just running, running, running. He came in the

house running. I said, 'Why are you running?' 'Because I was late,' and he knew he had to be home. I said, 'Don't ever run because someone will shoot you, the police will shoot you in the back if something happened. And they think because you running, you get shot. That happens to people.' I told him, 'You walk, boy! Or you call me and I will come get you. It always happens, all the time. It'll happen. You have to be a little more guarded, don't do that. You have to be guarded about certain things as a Black male. They will stop you for anything. If they stop you, see what they want, don't say no to them, then go on about your business. It's not worth going to prison, don't be with someone that is talking too much.' I try to tell him about that world too, because that's a mean world for him. He has to deal with it too with his friends. I just want to be realistic, that he is a target for this and 'don't run down the street. Don't put yourself in the situation that can harm you, get yourself shot or whatever. If you are going to be stopped, then be stopped.' A lot of Black males are just stopping [quitting on life], they'll stop you for whatever, they'll stop. I try to prepare him for that world too. 'There are precautions that you have to take because of who you are. Just deal with it.' We deal with it with a long talk. People who are talking bad—uh uh! 'You are going to have to deal with it so be ready for it.' I worry about that a lot. I hope if a situation comes up he'll remember what I said. He told me one time, 'The police are supposed to help you.' He said that not too long ago, about two years ago. I was so surprised that he thought like that. We still must be on guard.

I did not cover every aspect of Black male adult life in this chapter; that is, perhaps, impossible for one work. Yet, we find in this section that Black mothers teach lessons that encompass areas that are somewhat specific to Black manhood in the U.S., such as sex and interacting with police, and others that are not so distinct to manhood, such as compassion and respect. In neither the teaching nor the receiving of these lessons do we find that a mother is hindered by her sex or her experiences as a female.

In this second part of this section, I will juxtapose issues and concepts from the literature with findings in this project. We will analyze how these data either support those issues, concepts, and dynamics or negate them. We will examine the following areas that were extracted from the literature: the existence and function of othermothers and extended family support systems, the availability of role models, the notion that young males of Black single mothers often expect their sons to become "the man" in the household prematurely, and the provider role. Many of those issues appear in the literature as assertions without studies to support them, or they rely on outdated sources.

Some scholars (e.g., Sudarkasa, 1988) write about women-centered networks where bloodmothers and othermothers provide child care across blood or biological ties. When we examine these writings more closely, we find that most scholars use the works of Gutman (1976), who primarily focuses on slave families and/or Sudarkasa (1980, 1988) whose data essentially emphasize women-centered networks among Continental Africans, as evidence to support their assertions about othermothers currently existing in the United States. Consequently, there is a need to study this dynamic in more recent times given that Gutman's work was done in 1976 and Sudarkasa's work was primarily completed in 1980. In this project, we find some support for othermothers along the lines of biological or familial ties. In this first excerpt, Ms. Green, a single mother who became economically disadvantaged after her divorce, raised one of her sons for a majority of his life with an othermother present.

> At one point, we lived with Damien's aunt, my ex-husband's sister. She was very ill and asked us to live with her to assist her and we did that for five years. After that period of time, three years lapse and we came here [she now lives with her sister]. He has lived with a lot of support but it has always been a woman for most of Damien's life. So he has had two mothers, if you will, for probably 10 of his 20 years. So he wasn't left alone a lot.

In this second excerpt, we find Mrs. Myers, a married middle-class woman (middle class during the time of the interview) who depended on an othermother to help rear her son while she went away to school:

> I was in nursing school when I got pregnant so what happened, I dropped out in the middle of my senior year, he was born in March. I left the semester in January, and then I kept him until he was almost a year. Then my sister-in-law kept him for a year while

I went back and finished nursing school. So he was a toddler then. They had no other children in the house; it was just she and my brother and I think they did a very good job with him during that time. I was in the area, but my husband was in Northern California at the time, that's where we lived. I had to come back down here to finish nursing school because that's where I went. I'd go see him on the weekends, that's the kind of bonding I had with him early, which is not ideal but they were very nurturing to him.

Just as we find some examples of othermothers in this study, we find examples of strong extended family systems that these mothers use for financial, emotional, and parenting support. Moreover, a majority of these participants are involved in church, which also gives them emotional, spiritual, and sometimes parenting support. All of these mothers attest to some outside support in assisting them in raising their sons.

Notwithstanding these support systems, this study does reveal evidence of what Wilson (1995) said was the "increasingly persistent and prevalent social and personal difficulties [which] may now foment the demise of this valued family system" (p. 16). In addition to oppressive economic and political conditions, I wondered if migration and desegregation, specifically in Southern California, also contributed to the erosion of Black family support systems.

Mrs. Little, mother of two biological sons (40, 37), an adopted son she has raised since he was four (now age 15), and a daughter (32), and Mrs. Waters discuss the experience of some Black Southern Californian families being separated from their extended family systems. Both of these mothers' comments provide examples of families systems being diminished due to migration during the 1960s and '70s:

Mrs. Waters: My children grew up here. That is one disadvantage of growing up here. They did not get a chance of being in the surroundings of cousins and grandparents because we moved here and once we got married we left. So he was never around uncles, grandmothers, and grandfathers until vacation time. So around vacation time was when he was around family; and he did not experience them when they were small. He did not experience a lot of family activities.

Mrs. Little: We didn't have a lot of the grandmotherly type image or fatherly type image with them but in my preparing them I taught them lots of times the way it was when I was coming up because when I came up I had mother, father, grandmother, grandfather, uncles, and aunts who all lived right together and all took part in raising the children. I talked to them a lot about that, how I was raised and my brothers and my father raised my brothers. I took them to church, they went to church every Sunday.

Mrs. Fine, mother of two sons (3, 2 months), offers a more modern day experience. She and her husband live far from most of their family, and this is coupled with the prevalence of divorce in their families, which Wilson (1995) refers to as one of the social difficulties confronting Black families:

Interviewer: Are you involved in any support systems to help you in parenting?

Mrs. Fine: For myself in our family I would say, no. Probably within my family there is so many divorces, with my husband's parents. They're both divorced and my parents are both divorced so it's pretty much my husband and I raising our kids ourselves. We can go visit Grandma. We can't have a Thanksgiving dinner and have both grandma, grandpa, grandma, grandpa on both sides. It's either we are at grandma's house or we're at grandpa's house. When we are in the same area then we have to stay 15 minutes with this grandma and maybe 25 with that one because that's all we can tolerate. And it's 10 minutes here and there so it's really hard. Our family is so, I don't want to say dysfunctional. We talk about it but it's sad. We're way out in California, my husband is from Texas, I'm from Ohio so we really don't have that.

Embedded in this possible growing trend of deteriorating family support systems is the issue voiced by others (e.g., Wright, 1991) concerning the availability of appropriate Black male role models. While these data are saturated with examples of uncles, grandfathers, teachers, coaches, deacons, and other male professionals who acted as positive role models, some mothers report a concern that is rooted in the unavailability of Black family support systems. Underscoring this point about deteriorating family systems, especially in Southern California, and its connection to the accessibility of Black male role models is an excerpt from the group interview with relatively new and younger mothers.

Interviewer: Are there two other men outside your husbands that are in your sons' lives that you would say are good examples of manhood—besides your husbands?

Mrs. Fine: Within our family I can honestly say, 'No.' I have a brother and they have kinda fell off that righteous road and they're doing their thing.

Mrs. King: Yes.

Mrs. Owens: Yes.

Mrs. Ross: I understand that well maybe it is true with my sister, that there are people in the church because she and her husband, they associate more than my husband and I do at church. Outside of my husband, you're asking for two male figures that my son can look up to and use as examples. No, it's sad but no. I have two brothers and it's the same situation as Mrs. Fine. My oldest brother he doesn't even really believe in God and then my other brother was really on fire, so-to-speak, and he has totally fell off. At church everybody is kind of clique-ish, they have their own group of who they associate with and then my husband is really careful of who he hangs with and who he lets into his circle. Outside of my husband, there's only one and that's my sister's husband, my brother-in-law. There's only one. It's sad when you really think about it. It used to be in a community everybody was related, everybody was looking out for your child, everybody was trying to be an example. That's what I hear, that's what our parents and grandparents talk about. I can honestly say, no, and it's really sad.

It must be emphasized that although the separation of Blacks from their family support systems may have negative effects (e.g., a decreasing pool of available role models), this is not the cause of social ills facing Black communities. Other conditions, such as those mentioned by some of the mothers in the above excerpt and highlighted in the list of Black male statistics in Chapter 1, influence the accessibility of Black male role models. Moreover, this discussion is presented as a growing trend, not as the norm. A majority of these mothers have some family members living in close proximity, and the ones who do not have found ways, as much as possible, to re-create similar and useful support systems. Nevertheless, this dynamic desperately needs scholarly attention in the near future.

Some scholars (e.g., Randolph, 1995) report that in some cases, Black boys of single mothers are often asked to assume adult male responsibilities. Consequently, this causes some boys to negatively act out because of the strain of the adult role and the lack of opportunities to participate in age appropriate activities (Boyd-Franklin, 1989). This study reveals that some single mothers expected their oldest sons to assume adult responsibilities:

Ms. Green: The thing I did the most with Mike was that he had to assume a role of surrogate dad and everything as a young teenager. From the time he was 15, I also had a goddaughter living with me for three years. Mike pretty much ran my household. I worked two jobs, I brought home the checks, he banked them, he paid the bills, he made the budget. He did all those kinds of things. I think those things made him a better man.

Interviewer: At what age?

Ms. Green: Fifteen. I think that really helped him to be a better man and really, from an economic standpoint, to know early on how to treat and handle finances.

Mrs. Little: With my oldest son he did take on responsibility after he reached a certain age of trying to be that father image because he was about three and a half years older than the next son and about five years older than my daughter, so as he started reaching his teenage years, he was very mature in a lot of ways. He tried to take on that father image with the other two.

Interviewer: Did that change your relationship with him at all, him trying to take on that father image?

Mrs. Little: I had a lot more respect in a lot of ways for him as a teenager to take on more responsibility and go out and work when he was going to school to help out in the house. That was kind of what I wanted to see in both of them. That's how I tried to raise both of them.

Mrs. Eve: They had to be good strong young boys especially for Kyle, he's the oldest. I instilled that. When I say instilled, I was giving him confidence and standing strong behind him and pushing him to be the kind of person that I wanted as a man in my life, which I didn't have.

Interviewer: You said, 'You sat them down.' Did you wait until they were a certain age or when did these talks take place?

Mrs. Eve: I started with Kyle, my oldest son, when he was about four. My mother lived up the street and I would send him up to see my mother because my mother had heart trouble like me. I said, 'Go see Grandma,' and he would go up, and he'd say, 'Mother, I'm scared of the dog.' I said, 'Get you a stick and go right on by the dog, look him directly in the eye and he would not bother you.' I said, 'You a big boy, you the big boy in Mama's day.' This is the way I pushed him. One time when I was an unmarried mother, living right down the street from my mother, young, and I had the two kids, unmarried, and I told my oldest son Kyle that he had to be the man of the family. He had to be strong. If anyone comes to the house, he had to take a Daddy's place, as man. Someone would knock on the door, 'knock knock.' 'Who is it?' 'M'Dear, who is that?' That's what he would say. He was afraid. I said, 'Go answer that door. I told you, you had to be the man.' So he would do that. From then on, he would have to look after his little sister which was Alice, just a year between. Then when I got married and had other kids, he still had to be the man.

The degree to which each of these three sons had to assume adult roles is varied. Yet, the concept of the oldest male being expected to shoulder grown-up responsibilities is universal in all three examples. The extent that this had negative effects on the sons, although this clearly was not my focus of this study, was not evident. In fact, all three mothers see this dynamic as a positive learning experience for their sons. Moreover, not any of the sons report this as having negative effect on their lives. I asked Ms. Green's son Mike (27) directly about the responsibilities he had as a teenager. He said, "I never felt any pressure on me to be the man. I played sports and went out with my friends; my mom did a good job with that. The things that I did do, I think really helps me as a father today."

A possible defining variable in whether a boy has to assume adult responsibilities might depend on whether the mother has other men in her life. In the most extreme example in this present study, Mrs. Green did not really get involved with other men after her divorce and she also sought housing with other women in her family, all of whom prevented men to be in the presence of her sons. In this next example, Donald did not have to assume adult responsibilities. He says that his grandfather was the "man of the house."

Interviewer: Since you were with your mom all the time, sometimes with young boys there's pressure to become a man earlier. Was that the case?

Donald: No, I had friends who experienced that and actually my grandfather had to do that but no, I didn't have to do that. For most of my childhood we all lived in one big house. When I say we all, I mean my grandfather, my grandmother, my mother, sister, the two brothers, and her sister's son. I had a brother around so-to-speak, but we all lived in this big house, "Brady Bunch" kind of thing for all of our childhood up until I was about 10 or 11. I always saw a father figure. My grandfather didn't spend a lot of time because he was a working man, he worked all the time, but I saw a man in the house and I didn't have to even [assume the man of the house role] when me and my mother stepped all the way out on our own. I didn't have to try to become a man. I was allowed to still be the boy who was being raised by a mother who was strong, but she didn't try to push me past where she thought I needed to be for that time.

This phenomenon may not be limited to sons. It is also reported that the oldest daughter in single-parent families undertakes adult responsibilities and tasks (McLoyd & Wilson, 1990). Although I did not find harmful consequences in this study, this does not eliminate the potential risks described by others (e.g., Randolph, 1995).

As noted earlier, some scholars contend that, in the United States, manhood is equated with the ability to provide for one's family (e.g., Franklin, 1984). The mothers did not directly talk about the ability to provide as being an aspect of manhood. This concept may have been embedded in the dialogue concerning responsibility, which was the most pervasive aspect in respect to manhood characteristics. Although they do not necessarily link it to their mothers' teachings, the male participants overwhelmingly connect manhood to being able to provide. Here are a few examples:

135

Tony (15), Mrs. Piper's son.
Have a good job. It seems like it's going to be scary because in comes the bills, a lot of additional responsibilities and things like that. Characteristics just having a job, taking care of myself. That's about it.

Donald (29), Mrs. Miller's son.
To be a man of integrity and to always have a job, a job! To be able to stand on your own two feet.

Chapman (25), Mrs. George's son.
I thought that was important, to be able provide for the family. That was always key in whatever context, whether it was financially or whatever my limited knowledge, I knew I had to provide in some sort of way for the family.

Joshua (14), Mrs. White's son.
Responsible, stuff like that. They should be responsible, have a job, pay their bills.

In this last part, I'll report some of what we learned about the fathers of these sons. Fathers were not the focus of this inquiry, but one important idea about fathers was clear in my research: especially in cases where the boy's parents were married during his early years, the fathers, according to both mothers and sons, are well respected and have an immeasurable amount of positive influence on their sons' lives. These Black fathers, as is reported by many scholars (e.g., Hyde & Texidor, 1994), are highly involved in their sons' lives. On the other hand, fathers' involvement varied with sons who no longer lived with them due to divorce or separation. These next two excerpts are polarized examples showing the diverse levels of involvement by fathers who do not live with their sons.

Ms. Homes: His father and I are raising these kids together and we have agreed on what values we choose to instill in our kids so what I am saying to you is not just coming from me. I talk to his dad, we talk to each other about how we are going to raise them and this is what we agreed on. He's getting it from me and his father.

Mrs. Eve: I was kind of having a hard time with him and I told him to call his father because he was graduating from seventh to the eighth or the eighth to the ninth. I said, 'Call your Dad back to Louisiana and ask him to send you enough money to get an outfit for the graduation.' And I think that was when he made up in his mind he wanted to be a better person. He wanted to be a better Dad to his son if he ever had one, better than his Dad was to him. His father never sent him that money and that was pretty much the end of their relationship.

For the most part, in this study, separated or divorced fathers who lived near their sons were painted by both mothers and sons as having positive ongoing influential relationships with their sons. Fathers who lived a great distance from their sons, like in Mrs. Eve's son's case, were portrayed pejoratively.

A great deal of what was mentioned about fathers transpired in the context of single or separated mothers discussing mistakes they had made. Some mothers speak with great pride about keeping their sons' fathers in a positive light in front of their children. For example, Ms. Harris says, "I am proud of myself and thank God that I did not do that. I never kept them away from seeing their father. I never was negative. I would never do that either." Others discuss this as an area they would like to improve:

Ms. Evers: Well a couple of things. When I was going through about two years of breaking up with their Dad, I did have outbreaks of temper in front of them and I don't think that was good. We would fight and I would just be enraged and I would yell and say all sorts of things and I think that wasn't healthy. I have done a lot to try not to do that anymore.

Interviewer: Were you just angry or was it centered on their father? What was the problem?

Ms. Evers: I never thought of them seeing me attacking him. I thought of it like, I tell them not to fight, I tell them not to have temper fits and here I am doing it. And plus you hear and read that kids get scared when they see their parents fight and so I never thought of it, 'Oh, Mommy attacking Dad.'

Ms. Jones: At one point, because his dad and I divorced, he was playing the two of us against each other and it worked! I stopped all contact and because of that he felt he had so much power and got really rebellious. I am protecting him, thinking it was something his father did and it wasn't. We all suffered from that and I wished I involved his father, told him what was happening, what was said once I found out that things he was doing was not right.

Mrs. Mills: One more thing I want to tell you is I don't try to say too much about when you have problems with your spouse, to say to the children, when you have older children who are not there, still that's their father and it's the same thing, although it's not working for you, it still works for them. I always have to watch myself, sometimes I do bad. I am asking something and he says, 'Don't ask me this because it's really something I shouldn't know and talk to him [his father] about it.' That is one thing I work on, he'll tell you! 'Don't ask me that's between you and him, I don't know, Mom!'

How Are the Sons Doing?

Given the mothers' parenting styles and the everyday challenges facing Black families, how are sons doing? The mothers with adult sons report that their sons are very successful in their careers. The mothers speak highly of the parenting abilities of those sons who have children. The oldest son of one mother is in prison, and one other mother's son had a run-in with the law. He has,

139

in her words, "turned his life around." These two sons were the exception. Most sons are now ministers, Ph.D.s, college counselors, correctional officers, and service men. For the most part, mothers, especially lower and working class mothers, spoke proudly of the fact that none of their children ever used drugs or went to jail. The adult sons confirm their mothers' conclusions about the successful outcome of their lives.

Mothers who are currently raising sons in their home also report that their sons are doing fairly well in school and with friends, especially in the case of teenage boys. Two of the elementary boys' mothers say that their sons have Attention Deficit Disorder (ADD), which makes schooling, parenting, and socializing more challenging for their sons. However, this scenario is balanced with mothers and sons who report straight "A" grades.

The following comments are from the sons themselves. It is important to note that these following excerpts represent typical responses from the sons and that I found no correlation between marital or income status and the degree of life success experienced by the sons.

Tyri (10), son of Ms. Homes.

Interviewer: How are you doing in school?

Tyri: I'm doing OK in school.

Interviewer: What does OK mean?

Tyri: I'm doing great in school?
Interviewer: What does great mean? Are you making A's, F's, C's?

Tyri: I'm making A's and B's.

Interviewer: How are you doing with friends? Are
                 you getting along with people well?

Tyri: Yes.

Joshua (14), son of Mrs. White.
Interviewer: How are you doing in terms of school
                 and friendships, that kind of stuff?

Joshua: I'm doing pretty good, I got a 4.0 in grades.

John (16), mother is Mrs. Mills.
Interviewer: How do you think you're doing in terms
                 of school, in terms of friendships?

John: I'm doing good, I'm doing cool. I'm
                 not tripping off friends, not girls or
                 nothing. I have to find my own way.
                 I got a couple of true homeboys that I
                 kick it with. Other than that, there's
                 football and school.

Donald (29), son of Mrs. Miller.
Interviewer: How are you doing in life now?

Donald: Actually I'm doing all right. I've been
                 married five years in November. We
                 have a business and my wife is in this
                 business. I am a minister. We're both
                 trying to finish school and raising our
                 niece who is three years old. We've
                 had her for almost two years. We're
                 doing all right.

Kyle (40), son of Mrs. Eve.
Kyle: My mother taught me well. I am a good
                 father and I like my work in corrections.

Summary

In this chapter we discovered that Black mothers have many personal characteristics that are quite important in the mother and son relationship. Moreover, we find that these mothers are profoundly knowledgeable about current and historical issues surrounding Black males, which gives them a pragmatic insight about how to raise their sons. This chapter also reveals that Black mothers embrace an African-centered paradigm of manhood and masculinity. Finally, these mothers employ a number of techniques in order to teach their sons comprehensively about life, manhood, and adulthood.

As I talked to mothers, I discovered that the very characteristics that mothers thought were important for them to possess manifested and became part of their sons' character. This phenomenon can best be described by the saying, "whatever you sow, so shall you reap." Mothers planted seeds of respect, responsibility, honesty, and compassion, and are reaping the fruits of these teachings. I will close this chapter with a long excerpt, but it is one that best exemplifies the lessons.

It was Ms. Harvey who said, "Responsibility. That's number one for me." While I did not ask her to give me an example of how her son is responsible, she reflected the following story about her son. Throughout she talks about his strong sense of responsibility, even in the midst of a difficult situation:

He really loved her and I preferred that they got married myself. I wanted them too. People say,

'Oh they're too young, they don't know what they are doing.' I say some people get married at 30 and divorced at 32. My grandparents got married when they were 14 and 16. They had 14 kids and they are still married. People can always change. Give them an opportunity to see if they want to make it. Let them try. Who is to say it won't work. But it has to be their choice.

And they did. They made the choice. He told me he was happy and that made me glad. We talked about it later. I told him, 'I was really happy for you, for Sharon and for Asha. I think that is good, the best way to start out as a family. And if you love, which you say you do.' She called me on the phone and said that he was so much a part of her life and that he cares so much about her. They are on opposite ends, they are not together telling me this. This is a separate time. They will be O.K. If they make it, maybe it's because they wanted to and if anything happens in-between, well, you can't predict that. So I told him I was happy that he did make that decision. I think he was happy too. Then they decided that they were going to go there and get married in May, last May.

He decided and came to me and brought all these papers. He said, 'Mama, I am going into the service.' 'Oh you are?' Yes, because one, he needed money, he needed a job. He started working right after school. 'And also because the service will pay for my education.' I said, 'All right, you're thinking.' 'I will be getting a lot of benefits, medical and all and if I decide to get a house they will help me get a house.' I said, 'Um, my baby's been thinking along the lines of what he needs to do!' How can he find a job? He's only 16. They don't hire 16 year olds. Michael doesn't look 16, he looks 18, 19, but when he applied, on the thing, it says 16, they say, 'No.'

That was frustrating him because he was feeling like he can't make no money, couldn't buy anything for Sharon or the baby. He could not get a job.

I was proud of him because he found his way. 'Mom, it's not really what I want to do but I need to do it.' How proud can you be of someone that wants to go to UNLV to play on the football team but it didn't work out that way. 'I got a family and this is what I need to do.' He was being *so responsible* [emphasis is mine]. He brought the recruiting officer by and I said, 'I am going to talk to him.' The Marines came by, the Army came by—OK, let's check him out and see what is going on. He and Sharon and me sat down and asked them all these questions and at the end of it, she said, 'He was going into the National Guard.' I said, 'OK.' He is doing that.

Talk to him on the phone, it was sad to see him go but I was so proud of him that he made that decision and stuck with it because he knew he had two people depending on him to do right. And he did! I was proud, I was happy! He'll come back and all his letters say, 'Get me an application from here, or there.'
'
Mama, did you fill out that financial aid?' He never lets up. I don't mind that because that is what mothers do. So that makes me think when he gets back and gets in this world he is already planning on what he is going to do so he will be OK. I can't hope for anything better than that. I keep writing him telling him, 'Asha is getting big, Sharon misses you. She is trying to find a job,' so it's like what all couples that get married young have to do.
One thing he told me, sometimes you wonder how well did you do in raising your children, and you never know and something happens that really tests them as to what kind of character they have and he told me, 'Mama, I don't want to live off you guys. I just need a little help to get started.' How many parents don't? Sometimes kids need help from their parents just to get a boost. My mother helped us get our first house. She co-signed with us. Whatever I can do I will do and he knows that.

144

Chapter 5
Beliefs vs. Actions: A Paradox in Black Mothers' Lives and Popular Hegemony?

> Certainly black people have not talked enough about the importance of constructing patterns of interaction that strengthen our capacity to be affirming.
>
> bell hooks
> *Yearning* (1990)

Based on the testimonies presented in Chapter 4, Black women are capable on many levels of raising their sons to become men. Yet, many of them believe the popular notion that Black women cannot teach boys to become men. This apparent paradox will be the focus of this chapter.

Black Mothers Know the Time

In Chapter 4, I asked the following question: Do Black mothers know the time? I discovered that Black mothers are aware of the political and social issues that influence the lives of Black males. In fact, their insights often mirror the critiques of scholars (e.g., Hill, 1997) concerning the oppressive, unequal power relations in U.S. society. Like many scholars (e.g., Akbar, 1991), these mothers perceive American society to be anti-Black male and, in essence, anti-African.

Ms. Green said, "What I have done most is try to prepare my sons for the challenges that face them as Black men in a society that doesn't accept, see, or recognize Black men." This sentiment is held by most of the mothers. Black mothers understand that society emasculates Black males, either as a by-product of its oppressive dynamics or directly as a means of maintaining control.

The mothers are consciously aware of the fact that Black males are confronted with and must overcome debilitating stereotypes. Again, their insights are similar to analyses in the current literature (Hutchinson, 1994). All of the participants are concerned about the effects of stereotypes on their sons' lives and some had devised strategies to help them. For example, to protect them from the dangers of being stereotyped by police officers, many mothers did not let their sons wear certain clothes.

Much has been written about the negative effects of the Eurocentric educational system on African people that use miseducation as a means of oppression (e.g., Bush, 1997). Although he made his assertions about the schooling process in the United States during the early part of this century, Marcus Garvey captures the essence of what educational scholars, historians, and activists currently maintain about the educational system in the United States:

> The present system of education is calculated to subjugate the majority and elevate the minority. The system was devised and has been promulgated by agents of the minority. This system was carefully thought out by those who desire to control others for their benefit, and the disadvantage of others to the

extent that the others would not immediately rise into happiness and enjoyment of life simultaneously and equally with them. It was never originally intended to make all the people equal at the same time, and more so it was not intended to elevate the darker races to the immediate standard of the white races from whom the minority sprung to establish the system of education[.] All text books and general literature therefore were coloured [sic] to suit the particular interest of those who established the system of education, and the group they represent as against the interest of others whom they did not want to immediately elevate to their standard. (Hill, 1987, p. 263)

Jacob Carruthers contends that Blacks now face a two-pronged attack, *mis*education and *dis*education:

Today, we can identify two patterns of intellectual disruption used among African-Americans. First, there exists a very sophisticated system of mis-education aimed at a small Black elite. This is the same kind of mis-education that Carter G. Woodson, and Edward W. Blyden before him, wrote about. Essentially it is a schooling process through which Black people are taught to think and act in European ways.

The second pattern is actually a process of "dis-education" aimed at the Black masses. The disastrous experiences of Black students at public schools provide ample testimony to both the mis-education of the Black elite and the dis-education of the Black masses. In the midst of the tragedy, the mis-educated elite is unable to propose remedies while the dis-educated masses continue to experience pervasive, persistent, and disproportionate underachievement in comparison with their white counterparts. (1994, p. 45)

Working class mothers agree with Carruthers. They claim that schools are not concerned with the educational outcomes of their sons. They mention that schools commonly encourage their sons to take classes that do not prepare them for college.

All of the mothers know that Blacks have to work twice as hard as others in order to be successful. We find evidence of this phenomenon in the work of Julianne Malveaux (1988), who found that Black males often make $200 to $300 a month less than their White male counterparts working the same jobs, and the same is true of Black and White women. Multiply these figures over a lifetime and a Black male would have to either increase his hours or work another job to keep pace economically with White males. These figures give teeth to what Ms. Waters and other mothers say about Blacks having to work "doubly hard."

Lastly, we find that Black mothers are concerned about the availability of Black male role models. Ms. Jones says, "His biggest challenge as a male would be learning to be a male. He is around so many women." Some scholars (e.g., Akbar, 1991) also argue that the lack of appropriate Black male role models is problematic for Black communities.

Do Black mothers know the time? We find that Black mothers mirror the critiques of scholars concerning that nature and status of Black manhood in the United States. Black mothers are aware of the conditions confronting their sons and they are raising them accordingly.

Finding a Balance

Black mothers seek for their sons a middle point between traditional masculinity and traditional femininity. Some call this balanced approach to manhood and masculinity *African-centeredness* (e.g., Baker-Fletcher, 1996); others call it *androgyny* (Bem, 1984, 1987). Sandra Bem elucidates:

> Thus, for fully effective and healthy human functioning, both masculinity and femininity must be tempered by the other, and the two must be integrated into a more balanced, and more fully human, and truly androgynous personality. An androgynous personality would thus represent the very best of what masculinity and femininity have each come to represent, and the more negative exaggerations of masculinity and femininity would tend to be canceled out. (1987, p. 209)

This balance is most evident in my conversation with Ms. Evers and her sons. Ms. Evers does not want her sons to be a shark or a guppy.

Along these same lines, most mothers want their sons to be responsible. They want them to be as one mother says, "Responsible to himself." True to himself and "responsible to his community." Being responsible in an African-centered sense goes beyond the individual and his immediate family and is tied to a community (Akbar, 1991).

As found in the studies on Black males (e.g, Roberts, 1994), the mothers see spirituality as an important dimension of masculinity; spirituality is also a strong component of African culture. Specifically, the mothers most often connected spirituality with church, "God," and the Bible. Mrs. East said about her son, "I want him to be strong in his mind and strong in his heart." Akbar has an African-centered view of "strong in mind and heart."

> Intelligence, therefore, is intended to be nothing more than a servant to the higher being, or Divine Ka. In the ancient Kemetic [Egyptian] realm, intelligence was considered to be located in the heart. It is not only considered to be rational, but for also spiritual and ethical. Akhur perceives the principles of Maat. It permits a fusion between reason and attributes such as harmony, truth, compassion, justice, etc.
>
> In Ancient Kemet, the test of intelligence would unfold at the judgment of the deceased. When Anubis guides the deceased into the court of Ausir (judge of the Divine Ka), the deceased one's heart is placed on the scale of justice. One's intelligence is measured by whether or not the heart has been so lightened that it will not tilt a feather on the other side of the scale.
>
> If the test is passed, it means that one has used their intelligence to cultivate harmony in their ethical or moral being. One can achieve this feat by having used their intelligence to transform a corrupt society to a purified one...One should use their intelligence, not to feed passion, but to elevate and transcend it so that the heart becomes (en)lightened. (1994, p. 11–12)

In conclusion, scholars (e.g., Baker-Fletcher, 1996) contend that an African-centered or androgynous (Bem,

1984, 1987) model of masculinity is desired, fitting, healthy, liberating, African, and more humane than the Western model. We find that Black mothers are in tune with the push by scholars and leaders to develop and maintain a Black model of manhood that strikes the balance between masculinity and femininity. Again, I found that Black mothers are well prepared on many levels to raise their sons to become men. They possess the maturity needed to raise their sons well. They are acutely aware of challenges that are specific to Black men. Their goals for manhood are in harmony with ancient African principles and current philosophies about the duality of masculinity and femininity in all human beings.

A Paradox?

Mother after mother, some of them for hours at a time, provided endless examples of how they are cultivating within their sons the qualities, characteristics, morals, and behaviors consistent with their definitions of manhood. Yet, many of these women, some without direct questioning from me, voiced their belief that a woman could not show a boy how to become a man. Again the mothers are in complete agreement with many scholars. We will compare Mrs. Miller's statement, which was a response to a direct question, to this idea that mothers cannot raise boys to manhood. I will use bold type to underscore parallelism.

Interviewer: What is it about being a woman that makes you feel you are less qualified to raise a male into manhood? What is it that you don't have?

Mrs. Miller: I am not a man, I am not a man. When it comes to identity. When a male is raised in an all female situation pretty much there is something that they lose. Not that they are a worse man or can't be a good man, they can't be a strong man, I just think it enhances the picture when there is a strong role model. They are at home with the female, they go to school up until high school pretty much with all females, they see a nurse when they go to the doctor, so their whole image of professionalism or someone in a caring position is basically a female and so I think the feminine side of a man is there very much because they are around females a lot but the male side which helps them to be balanced, helps them to have somebody to emulate [is not there]. For example, when they are going to be a husband, I can't teach my son to be a husband. I can see or he can see what kind of husband I have now, but at that time he didn't have that role model and it's hit and miss.

"Their teachers in the first five years of school, from kindergarten to the 4th grade are usually women. If they get in trouble, a female teacher will send them to a principal—often a woman—who will report their behavior to a female head of household…Is it no wonder that these young boys begin early either to develop an attitude of hating women or else to emulate women even to adopting their mannerisms? Neither result is desirable or acceptable.

"...try as they may, and well-meaning as they may be, women can not teach black boys to be men. The boys need close association of legitimated Black role models, and the ear lier this becomes a reality, the better-adjusted the child will become." (Wright, 1991, p. 22)

I interviewed Mrs. Miller early in the schedule. When she and some of the other mothers, who were also among the first to be interviewed, stated their own inability to model manhood I just listened and did not probe for an interpretation. However, during the latter interviews, I began to probe, in some instances, confront mothers about this issue that I thought was a contradiction between their actions and their beliefs. In this next excerpt, I confront the four relatively new mothers (Mrs. Fine, Mrs. King, Mrs. Owens, and Mrs. Ross) who participated in the interview.

Interviewer: We started off talking about what you could show your son as a woman, how are you going to teach them to be adults, men. Now you are saying 'only my husband can do this.' 'I can't do it!' Now I am wondering what do you think you cannot teach your son?

All:	How to be a man of God, dealing with society, walking like a man, talking like a man.
Mrs. King:	In my opinion, it doesn't matter what we tell them, they will do what they see, children do what you do so I cannot teach him. I am a woman, he's a man, we're different. I can only teach him self-love from a woman's point of view. Maybe it is different for the different genders...In a sense where integrity and self-love and all that, it's not that it is different, but it is a different point of view coming from a woman. I'll teach him how to be gentle. In this society he can't be too gentle because he will be knocked all over the place. My husband will sock him, I just can't punch him. God didn't build me like that. We as women come more from an emotional feeling type what we put into our sons. We all know that women are much more into emotions than men. The father cannot teach them how to really touch and feel and that sensitive side. Men just don't have, the men I know, you rarely see a man cry, for whatever reason, and come out and admit that he's crying. They still gotta see a man doing it, they got to see a man getting up going to work everyday. They got to see a man holding his wife. You tell somebody that all day, children are just modeling what they see. I can tell them all day.
Interviewer:	Does a child have the ability to transfer what he sees you do as a woman, like

154

being responsible, into what he is supposed to do as a man?

Mrs. King: Maybe that could happen, but I think—

Mrs. Ross: I think, to go along with what Mrs. King is saying, I know I wouldn't be able to teach my son completeness by myself. Women are more emotional creatures so therefore we can tell them all these things and we can try to teach them all these things but it would be from a different point of view from their fathers. They need to see both, they need to see both parties. Children who are raised in broken homes, not to say that they are not ever complete, but I'll speak concerning myself. I believe that I still have work that needs to be done on myself. I think that children that are raised in broken homes, to come to that point, that I am a whole person, I'm a whole person by myself, I don't need somebody to make me a whole person. We get to that later down that road than children who are raised in a family where the mom is there and the dad is there most of the time. Men still can stray away and go their own way even after they had been in a home where both parents are there and the parents have done all they can do to make sure the kids go the right way.

Mrs. Fine: We also have to realize that there are men issues, things men go through, life passages. And also women, whether it be pregnancy, or gang banging or drugs, there are certain issues that girls go

155

through. That is why I didn't want a girl. I didn't want to deal with pregnancy, puberty. Honestly, I don't want to deal with a little girl. Maybe I'm being terrible when I say this but I can fall back on my husband to deal with the male issues whenever it may be, and that is something I cannot do. I am not a man, I couldn't tell him, from an outside person, 'I don't know honey, you are going to have to go to your dad for that.' We are two different, separate genders. I may not be able to give that to my son. I'm sure I couldn't. With his father being there he can say, 'That's normal,' or we need to go this route or his father may know a little about it. Example, since he has been down that road of using drugs and no father in the house, he can tell my brother more, 'Son you don't want to go down that road.' My mother, she's just like yelling and tripping and she's trying to make him mind this and that, but when they start becoming a man and they're not virgins no more there are issues that my mother can't deal with. She needs my father now in the house with him for me and my sister. We didn't need to fall back on my dad because my mother understood the issues of pregnancy or whatever. My brother needs my father now more than ever. He is starting to go on the passage way. I can't really, you can, but I would prefer not to raise my son by myself because there are certain things that Mommy can't do for him.

There is much to be dissected in the dialogue with the group of mothers; however, we will move to one additional excerpt and then respond to some common themes that the mothers talked about. Within the first minute of her interview, Ms. Green said, "They cannot teach, this is my opinion, but I don't believe a woman can teach a young person to be a man. I don't believe that they can." I did not ask a question that warranted that response. Perhaps she was responding to the title of this project. The following comment was made later in the interview. Ms. Green is a woman with whom I am somewhat familiar. Therefore, we both felt comfortable having this intense conversation.

Interviewer: I'm having trouble here. I'm hearing two things. I'm hearing you tell me your ideology, that women can't do this. Then I'm hearing these stories, great examples. You told the characteristics of a real man. You told me responsibility, and this and that, then I asked you, 'How do you show responsibility? How do you show caring? How do you show this?' And you have given me examples. Then your son is telling you that he has learned these things from you. But you still have this ideology that a woman cannot raise her son to become a man. I'm asking you, What is it that you can't teach?

Ms. Green: There are things that you can't teach them—like you can't teach them—

Interviewer: Such as?

Ms. Green: I can't tell my son what it feels like. I can sit down with a young girl and I could say this feeling that you have, whatever this is inside, is what happens when a woman is at this age and these are the things that motivate a woman, all those are things you have hormonally. I can't do that with a male and I think that is the kind of way I was meaning that. I can't do those kinds of things with them. I go and get the books and I sit down with them.

Interviewer: You may not know what exactly it feels like inside, what does that really have to do with anything?

Ms. Green: I guess that is my way, I still believe that even in raising our children, especially a male needs both parties to have the balance. I guess that is what I mean when I say that. Mike wasn't so much, he got all the basic stuff in a balance. I think it was enough to sustain him, but Damien, he didn't have that balance. I could tell when a guy was raised by a woman.

Interviewer: How's that?

Ms. Green: They are usually a little more effeminate in their behavior. They usually talk more like a woman; from a feminine standpoint. Men tend to make more choices, I believe, than a woman does. A woman kind of fixes on a point and that's it. I think men are a little more easier to go from one side to the other. More readily accepts something where a woman doesn't. I think those are things that show in a person that is raised by a woman.

Interviewer: Is that bad?

Ms. Green: I don't think it's bad. I think even when I say I could not teach my sons to be a man, that's not even bad. I think it's sorrowful to me because I feel like my children were a statistic, part of the norm of what you see of not being raised by a two-person household and their dad ended up a being a person who was absent and that saddens me.

Interviewer: What are your sons lacking because they didn't have a man?

Ms. Green: I don't think that Mike is lacking anything. In fact, it probably gave him more of an ability, more of a drive to parent better and to be a better husband and all of those kind of things. But with Damien, there is something mentally he feels he is lacking. I think it will be something that Damien will work out for himself.

Interviewer: What is Damien missing?

Ms. Green: The relationship with a male.

Interviewer: What is Damien missing of who he is because he had a woman raising him? He certainly does not act effeminate.

Ms. Green:	I don't know. I think, 'Would he be a better person? Would he be a better balanced person?' Probably. Seeing things from more than one viewpoint. Basically that is what really happens in a house. You see things from two viewpoints because you have two people with two different viewpoints.
Interviewer:	How is that different? You said he had another mother in the household?
Ms. Green:	Because we would see things the same.
Interviewer:	All the time?
Ms. Green:	Well, most of the time, not all the time. Between Carol and I it would depend on what it is, if it had anything to do with discipline. No, we are not on the same wavelength because she'll turn around and say just let them do it. She'll leave and excuse him and say go on and do it.
Interviewer:	Which are two points of view.
Ms. Green:	Right, that's true.
Interviewer:	So I'm asking—
Ms. Green:	I told you, I think it's probably more of something with myself. It's more of a hang-up with me.
Interviewer:	I'm not saying you're wrong, I am saying—
Ms. Green:	I think as a woman, I want to share the

160

responsibility so whatever happens here, however this whole scenario turns out, maybe I don't want it by myself, responsibility.

When I juxtapose the sentiments embedded in the previous conversations with the findings in Chapter 4, even when I compare some of these statements against the mothers' very own statements, there appears to be a paradox. Pointing out this incongruent dynamic yielded essentially three responses:

1. Women do not know about male sexuality and are therefore unequipped to instruct males.
2. Women produce effeminate males.
3. "Women are not men" and therefore are unable to teach boys certain aspects of manhood.

Let us explore these issues. We found that some mothers are very direct, open, knowledgeable, and effective concerning male sexuality, while some were a little more apprehensive. The crux of this issue rests, not in an inherent inability of mothers, but in the willingness of a mother and a son to engage this issue. Sons who participate in sexual training sessions with their mothers (additional research is needed in this area) may be better prepared to deal with all of the issues, especially what a woman expects from a man regarding courtship, romance, and intercourse. Thus, whether a woman perceives herself as

161

being able to instruct her sons in sex depends more on personality barriers than her womanhood or motherhood. The issue of effeminate males is of great concern in Black communities. This is due in part to a belief that hyperfemininity and hypermasculinity are counterproductive in Black communities. What also makes this a major issue is that effeminate characteristics in males are equated with homosexuality. When this is linked to homophobia and the decreasing pool of male role models and accessible mates for Black women (due to a variety of political, social, and demographic factors), then we can understand the intensity of emotion permeating beliefs about this issue.

According to the participants in this project and those who engage in heated debates on Black radio stations, in magazines, and in conferences across the U.S., Black women and mothers are directly to blame for creating effeminate Black males. However, the findings of this project do not support this notion that Black mothers, married, single, or those living in households with many women, cause effeminate behaviors in males. None of the male participants lack(ed) the benefit of older males positively influencing their lives. In general, boys always have male role models in their communities, whether positive or negative. If we believe that femininity is a behavior or quality that can be taught, then this ability, like the capacity for mothers to teach their sons about sexuality, transcends motherhood and is dependent more on the personality of each mother.

What if a male infant was born and raised on an island where there were only three women? Would the male grow up to be effeminate? Would the degree of masculine and feminine behaviors and characteristics exhibited by the male depend on the degree they manifest in any of the adult females? Or, is there something else within the male that will innately drive him toward a masculine disposition despite the influence of the females?

I was up late one night and the television was on, but I really was not paying attention to it. My interest was piqued, however, when someone said that they had decided at birth that their child would be female; thus, the parent had the penis severed. Because I tuned in late, I never did catch the reason why this occurred. Although I missed most of the show, I gathered that doctors were checking back with several patients, now four to six years old, who had suffered this particular procedure as infants.

Some doctors on the show suggested that these children were not successful at being girls or females. The young females exhibited what they called "tomboyish" behaviors. This is despite the fact that these children had been completely socialized as girls, which encompassed how they were dressed, how their family and the world interacted with them, their potty training, and any and all aspects of life imaginable. Is a girl's "tomboyishness" or a boy's "effeminateness" evidence of nature's influence, social programming, or is there a third explanation that has been ignored by the academy?

Prodded by the television show, I pursued related topics and came across the works of John Money, a researcher who has spent the last 48 years studying and writing about (more than 30 publications) hermaphroditism, sex, and gender issues. His latest work, *Gendermaps: Social Constructionism, Feminism, and Sexosophical* (1995), provides an overview of his earlier works. (When quoting Money, I will indicate "cited in" to distinguish quotes from earlier works that have been included in the 1995 text.)

Money learned a lot about gender differences from his study of hermaphrodites, which began in 1952 with dissertation research. He found that "masculine and feminine inclination, outlook, and behavior could not be automatically regulated by either the genetic or gonadal sex, nor by any other single anatomical or physiological variable of sex..." (1995, p. 20). Consequently, there was a need to forego previous prevalent definitions of sex as male and female and create a list of prenatally determined variables of sex that were independent of one another. After creating a list of five, then six variables, finally a list of seven was completed. In this list the last two presented are also the last two formulated: chromosomal sex, gonadal sex, internal and external morphological sex, hormonal sex (prenatal and pubertal), postnatal determinate (the sex assignment and rearing), and gender role (1995).

To better understand his conclusions about nature and nurture, let's first explore Money's term "gender role":

> By the term, gender role, we mean all those things that a person says or does to disclose himself or herself as having the status of boy or man, girl or woman, respectively. It includes, but is not restricted

164

to sexuality in the sense of eroticism. Gender role is appraised in relation to the following: general mannerisms, deportment and demeanor; play preferences and recreational interests; spontaneous topics of talk in unprompted conversation and casual comment; content of dreams, daydreams, and fantasies; replies to oblique inquiries and projective tests; evidence of erotic practices and, finally, the person's own replies to direct inquiry. (1955; cited in 1995, pp. 21–22) Money clarifies his position on gender-role acquisition:

> Chromosomal, gonadal, hormonal, and assigned sex, each of them interlinked, have all come under review as indices which may be used to predict an hermaphroditic person's gender—*his* or *her* outlook, demeanor, and orientation. Of the four, assigned sex stands up as the best indicator. *Apparently, a person's gender role as boy or girl, man or woman, is built up cumulatively through the life experiences he encounters and through the life experiences he transacts* [emphasis mine]. Gender role may be likened to a native language. Once ingrained, a person's native language may fall into disuse and be supplanted by another, but it is never entirely eradicated. So also a gender role may be changed or, resembling native bilingualism may be ambiguous, but it may also become so deeply ingrained that not even flagrant contradictions of body functioning and morphology may displace it. (1955; cited in 1995, p. 21)

Thus, Money mostly aligns with the primacy of nurture in the development of a masculine gender role. His conclusion that gender roles are not easily mutable and are essentially indelible by a child's first birthday, leaves the door open, however, for nature and other influencing factors. Money writes that "thinking people have long recognized the integrative unity and interdependence of what is contributed to the development from each side of the polarity. One cannot exist [nature or nurture] without the other" (1995, p. 35). Thus, returning to our fictitious island boy, we cannot assert with assurance his masculine or feminine outcome.

Before going on to the third issue in this section, there is one other variable besides nature and nurture that I have been alluding to throughout this discussion, which is spirituality. Do our souls have a gender? Akbar (1994) recognizes male and femaleness to have a place outside of biology and socialization that he calls *energy*. "Life is a cooperative process. It is a process that brings together the energies of male and female" (p. 26). To what degree does our soul, spirit, or spiritual energy influence our manifestation of gender roles? Although this question is beyond the scope of scientific inquiry and thus this project to a certain extent, the question is valid and deserves further study.

Turning to the third issue raised by the mothers in this project—"Women are not men" and "I am not a man"—Money's work is helpful. Granted, men and women are different. The following is Money's list of behavioral differences:

166

- General kinesis: muscular activity and the expenditure of energy, especially in vigorous outdoor, athletic, and team sport pursuits.
- Competitive rivalry and assertiveness for higher rank in the dominance hierarchy of childhood.
- Roaming and territorial boundary mapping or marking.
- Territorial defense against intruders and predators.
- Guarding and defense of the young.
- Nesting or homemaking.
- Parental care of the young, including doll play.
- Sexual positioning: mounting and thrusting versus presenting and enveloping.
- Erotic arousal: dependence on visual versus tactual stimuli. (1980; cited in 1995, p. 39)

Do any of these differences, along with a woman's biological uniqueness (such as the ability to menstruate, carry a fetus, and nurse a child), translate into a woman's ability to raise male children into manhood? According to many of the women in this study and others, the answer is no. They believe that the innate characteristics and behaviors in men qualify men solely for the job of bringing boys into manhood. For example, leading rites-of-passage expert R. Johnson gives some credit to Black mothers for socializing young boys, but he strongly maintains that "A mother could do a lot of things for boys, but when he gets ready to cross the bridge from boyhood to manhood, only a man could pull him across" (personal communication, June 8, 1997). Johnson and I had a 15 minute discussion between one of his manhood training workshops in which I respectfully sought him out to help me understand what it is about women, outside of individual personalities and experiences, that rendered them incapable of rearing a boy into manhood. He finally concluded, after I dismissed a few of his assertions, that "perhaps we do not even have the words to express it, but it is there."

Perhaps Johnson, the mothers, and the scholars are contending that there is something that men uniquely possess that allows them to bring boys into manhood. Surely, a social and spiritual rationale exists behind the ancient African practice of separating the males for male only rites-of-passage. Nevertheless, in all of the works I have read, the interviews I have conducted, and the intellectual debates with scholars, colleagues, and friends I have engaged in, no one has been able to name what "it" is that leaves men inherently capable of bringing boys into manhood. *The findings of this study certainly do not support such a conclusion.* Out of respect to my participants and others, and recognizing my limited ability to comprehend the vastness this study entails, I have created Figures 1 and 2.

Figure 1 graphically depicts the mothers' statements and findings in the literature about male-female influences on a boy's life. It is based on the African-centered model of manhood that incorporates both feminine and masculine qualities. The region to the left represents the aspects of manhood that possibly only fathers (men) can teach. The region to the right represents the aspects of manhood that possibly only mothers (women) can teach. The region of intersection represents the areas in males' lives that both mothers (women) and fathers (men) can influence to cultivate manhood. This region represents most of what a boy needs to know, possess, and master in order to reach manhood.

Figure 2 includes the community's influence on male development (the region at the bottom). Possibly there are aspects of manhood only a third party can teach, such as a mentor, role model, coach, teacher, or minister. Mrs. East makes the point:

> Going to church, seeing other brothers, I think keeping positive people in his life is a good help, especially like his teacher, he loves his teacher. All those good influences, the people here that he really likes. Those people are special to him. I think that is sometimes more important than even me, because there are things I can't teach him. So I welcome anything that is going to help. Children tend not wanting to listen to you half the time anyway. 'You don't know nothing.' But it's nice to hear from someone else what I said. 'Wow, you really did really know what you were talking about!' I need all the help I can get with my son.

Figure 1

Manhood Development Involving

Mothers (Women) and Fathers (Men)

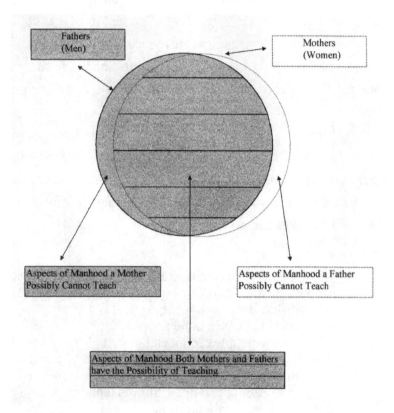

Figure 2

Manhood Development Involving

Mothers, Fathers, and the Community

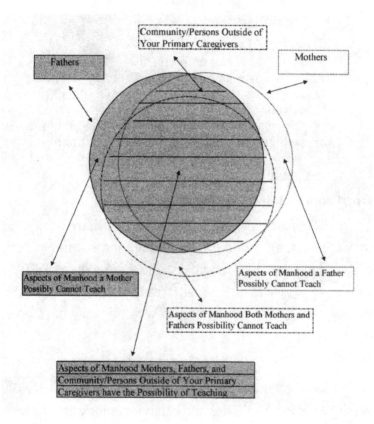

In Figure 2, the African adage "It takes a village to raise one child" is shown to have pragmatic value. When a community comes together to create, change, build, or raise a boy into a man, a transformative spiritual energy is created. Perhaps that is what is meant by Matthews 18:19–20:

> Again I say unto you, That if two of you shall agree on earth as touching any thing that they shall ask, it shall be done for them of my Father which is in heaven.
> For where two or three are gathered together in my name, there am I in the midst of them.

One People, Heterogeneous Lives

The participants in this study are married, single (never married), divorced, separated, and a combination of those states. Household incomes ranged from $0 to $130,000 per year, yet no pattern developed along these demographic lines. Hill explains why this may have been the case:

> Furthermore, it is important to recognize the diversity of values, attitudes and behavior among groups who are in similar socioeconomic levels. Many classic studies of the black poor revealed that low-income blacks are not monolithic and exhibit a wide range of values, attitudes, and child-rearing practices. (1997, p. 82)

Contrary to the findings of Hetherington (1991) and others, my project did not produce evidence of negative outcomes in sons based on income level or the marital state of the mothers. In other words, poor, single mothers are equally able to produce in their sons the African-centered characteristics and behaviors of manhood as wealthier, married mothers. As long as mothers are aware of the social oppressions against Black males and develop within their sons such qualities as responsibility, spirituality, honesty, and integrity, Black boys can become strong men under the guidance of a Black woman.

Mothers continue to be the first teachers of children, boys and girls. In the traditional nuclear family model, fathers generally work outside the home and mothers work inside the home. As a result, the mother has the greatest opportunity to influence the development of her children. Now that half of African American families are single-mother headed, are mothers now incapable of doing what they would have done had the traditional nuclear model been in place? Perhaps her task has been made more challenging, but as the evidence in this study suggests, the Black mother is certainly not incapable of raising her sons to become men.

Challenges to Black Motherhood

Europeans have declared war on African people (Jones, 1992), and Africans in America are nothing more than prisoners. These oppressive conditions make mothering and fathering difficult. Black males are especially targeted for destruction and this is the case whether they are raised by a single mother or one who is married. Consequently, the horrible statistics presented in Chapter 1 are not a result of incompetent and failing Black mothers, but rather an outright attack against every and all things African.

The double-edged sword of sexism and racism (Collins, 1990) works to de-center, devalue, and disempower Black mothers and womanhood. Like miseducation (Woodson, 1977), racism and sexism may cause self-hatred within women and hatred of women within males.

Economic conditions make mothering Black males a formidable task. Although the findings of this project and the work of Clark (1983) present evidence of successful child rearing in the face of economic constraints, still, some mothers are not able to spend much time with their children because of the need to work outside the home. This is an issue for all mothers of all income levels, whether married or single.

Although families of all races and classes face challenges on a daily basis, Black mothers must deal with so much more. Circumstances are more to blame for undesirable conditions facing Black communities than any lack in Black mothers. Nor should single Black women be scapegoated for her singleness, which is a symptom of larger problems.

I began this book not wanting to fall into the trap of blaming Black mothers for problems facing their communities. Likewise, because Black mothers were the focus of this research, it may appear that we have fallen into another trap of giving mothers all the credit for raising their sons. As discussed in Chapter 2, there are many sociological factors that contribute to the development of boys. Nevertheless, we found that mothers are not to blame, and given the statistics reported in Chapter 1 that are mostly a result of circumstances discussed in this section, **Black sons do not only need their fathers, but they also need otherfathers, othermothers, uncles, aunts, mentors, teachers, ministers, all-Black male schools, and all-Black male rites-of-passages.** And I would argue that Black girls need the same kind of intervention and prevention.

With respect to the intangible or indescribable "it," which I describe as aspects of manhood that mothers or fathers possibly cannot teach (Figures 1 and 2), I suggest that Black mothers make a list of all the areas of a man's life. This exercise will be useful for single and married mothers of sons. The following is a sample list of subjects, but feel free to add your own:

Spirituality	**Surviving/Protection**	**Cooking/Cleaning**
Love	**Economics**	**Black History**
Romance	**Health/Nutrition**	**Basic Repairs**

Under each heading, being as specific as possible, answer the questions who, how, what, when, and how often. For example, under spirituality answer the following questions: Who is teaching your son? What is being taught? How is spirituality being taught? When is it being taught? How often is it taught? If you find that you are unable to provide answers, or only one person doing the teaching, you have probably discovered the tangible "it" that is missing from your son's life. You must find the materials, individuals, and organizations to fill the vacancy. Your inability to fill these vacancies by yourself has nothing to do with your femaleness from what I have discovered. However, your ability to find the resources to fill what is missing could have an immeasurable influence on your son's development into manhood.

Chapter 6
Raising Black Males: Advice from Mothers and Sons

In the final pages of this book, I have included advice from mothers and sons on how to raise Black males. The data is raw—uncoded, uncategorized, and uninterpreted—but possibly useful to somebody.

Mrs. Waters, mother of a son (32) and a daughter (25).
Build trust, and be there for them. Make time.

Ms. Harvey, mother of two sons (17, 13).
Stay in their business. Never give up, they are your children, they really are. Let them know you really do care and there's nothing wrong in saying 'I love you' and that's why I am like I am. I really care about you. Even though life is hard for parents, for mothers, it's hard raising a male but I tell them how I feel as a female so they understand women a little more. I am a crying person and they have seen me cry before. They have made me cry before and I have no problem with that. Because when I cry they cry because they know they hurt me and there's nothing wrong with that. They have to stop thinking that women have to be super woman, they don't have to be like that.

More than likely, boys love their mothers. It's hard to give up their mothers and there is a connection there I think and should be there. They have to hold on to them, even though they're grown, they are still your babies, your children. I don't care, that's my baby. Don't give up. Be strong and at the same time be caring and let them know that's how you are. Give them a little room, you know how they can be mouthy a little bit. My kids never curse, I never heard them out. I never had to beat them or curse them and I don't think that is necessary to raise kids to be strong or respectful. You can get your point across. I stayed the same before I got the divorce as I was after the divorce. I made myself promise when this happened that I wouldn't let my kids suffer because of our situation. Whatever your situation is you know what you want from your kids and your situation changes, that doesn't mean the situation changes for your kids. You have to stick with that.

Mrs. Mills, mother of a son (16) and a daughter (18).

Talk to your children. And keep talking to them even if they don't want to hear it. Keep talking to them and always tells them they can be whatever they want to be and that's true. They have to realize that they do have some obstacles, there's nothing that they can't do. Black males have some special challenges because they have to deal with the threat, to me, from the White man; they can meet that. They really have it and you have to keep telling a child that they have it and when they show things that they do.

Point out people and things that have happened and show people doing: 'He's not sitting there waiting for someone to hand him a check and making excuses that the White man is keeping us down and all that stupid stuff.' Nobody keeps you down, you keep yourself down. As long as you're healthy, you keep trusting in God.

Number One, that you always have to keep talking to them about God and if you stop praying, you lose a lot because it keeps me, because I can only do so much but I don't have the perfectness in me. But if you believe in God, you believe in Jesus Christ, then you will make it. I always make them come and pray and talk about the Bible and stuff together. Keep them in church, keep God in their lives. They have to know God, because God has something to give them that people on this earth can fall back on.

Be there for them and just always encourage them that they can be what they want, anything they want, even what people think they can't be. I met one young man, he said that people never told him he was smart and that he is.

John (16), mother is Mrs. Mills.

Sometimes kids are a little weird. Sometimes it's the kids, sometimes it's the parents. There are a couple of parents that are cool, they are in their younger '30s and some parents are kinda old but cool. Talk like younger people talk and they can understand stuff better.

179

Ms. Green, mother of two sons (27, 20).

Teach the things that are important and don't focus on things that are not. Humbleness is so important. That is a main characteristic particularly in a Black male. How to love, how to nurture themselves, others. Knowledge is so important. If I had to just give you one thing, respect. If I had to pick one, that would be it. There are so many things that are important. I think the most important thing is to be loved first so that they are able to love. There is so much to do with children. I don't know if it ever stops. If you can accomplish those few things then you've made a pretty well-rounded person. If they can be respectful, if they can be humble, if they have knowledge of what they're dealing with, and knowledge of everything around as much as possible. If they know how to love, how to be loved. So many people don't know how to be loved, in particular, men. I think a lot of us don't know how to show it—women.

I think it's important for them to know that they are needed. The importance of being needed. The importance of the role of fathering and mothering. Being a wife. It is so necessary. It's not a lot of time, I would tell a young mother that—it's not a lot of time. Nothing you do is too soon to get started on it, loving, teaching, humbleness, respect, none of that is too soon at an age. There's no need to wait, not necessary. I think consistency is very important. I think above all is a way to effectively do it all without feeling like you haven't.

I conclude the only thing that would have helped out a lot is if a young mother or a young wife spends time with those who have been through the experiences. And in my case, I didn't do a lot of that because I am a very private person so I didn't share. A lot of my dilemmas could have been solved had I been a sharing person. A lot of mine was embarrassment, just being embarrassed over my whole situation and being shocked from it. I think I would give a young woman advice of not being that way. Get help, talk, from older and wiser people who have been through the experiences. Listen to the experiences, take in as much as you can like a sponge because when you need it, it will come.

Mrs. Walton, mother of three sons (31, 30, 21) and a daughter (19).

I think women need to keep their boys involved in activities, live their life as an example. It's good for a male child to have a male example but moms can raise men to be men because there are a lot of qualities and a lot of things that we interject that a man from a man's point of view doesn't see.

Make sure that the male child has exposure to positive male role models whether it is a grandfather, uncle, or someone that they can bond with. Where they can see from a male point of view and those things that we instill could be the softer side. Two parents together can do a lot because of two points of view in the midst but if you don't

181

have that male point of view, you need to make sure that the child has the exposure with other men as much as possible. Sometimes if there's family sports or other activities where all guys or something like that.

Mrs. Black, mother of four sons (47, 44, 40, 36) and three daughters (52, 40, 37) (two sons and one daughter are stepchildren).

It's harder today than probably ever. I would say you have to have some kind of moral conviction, you have to set your own limits, let them know what you will and will not tolerate. Stick to your guns and pray a lot! Today there are so many forces. Challenges are more greater today so I think a mother would have to pray and really start very early guiding them in the right direction and hope they stay there.

Today the peer pressure is greater, there are things out there challenging children today that were not there yesterday. If my kids came in the evening, or someone said they were going to ride their bike to the park or ride to the Mission Hills and do something, there was no reason for me to ever feel that the child would not return home. That somebody would be knocking on the door saying that they were found shot, or this or that. There was no reason to think that. I could send one of my children walking to the market, we have a market right up here in this little center, I could send a child and feel comfortable that he would get to the market and get back home.

Today you can't do that. It's a greater challenge but the parenting skills remain the same.

I still say you have to spank. I don't go for the 9-1-1 thing. If the parent needs to grab the child and set him straight, I say set him straight! That is the parent's prerogative. Train that child, set limits, and pray. It's harder but I think you can be successful. I still go with the same thing what we did a hundred years ago in bringing up children.

Mrs. East, mother of two sons (12, 2) and one daughter (9).

Always teach them what's right and show them what's right. If you're not living your life right, you can for sure expect a sorry adult child. If you live your life right and you do right by that child, when I say 'do right' I don't mean spoiling them and buying them everything they want because you have a guilt trip.

Mrs. Piper, mother of a son (15).

Encouragement, constantly instilling qualities, 'you can make it, you can do things.' I don't think there is a limit of what you can do especially if you have a gift or talent and don't be afraid to try things and most of all listen. Listen to your children, have time to listen. If you don't listen, then someone else is and giving them advice. He is going to be 16 in April. In a few years he's going to be gone. This is a critical time. When he was younger it was easy, now I just have to be patient and hang in there.

Tony (15), mother is Mrs. Piper.

Try to keep a close relationship with them like with your daughters. Always stick by him, don't never let him stray too far away because if they do it causes a lot of pain and suffering. Discipline-wise, if I were a father, I would whip my child until he was 18 and out of the house just to teach him certain things, but stick by your son, your child, don't let him stray too far away. Keep a close relationship.

Mrs. Myers, mother of a son (36) and two daughters (35, 31).

I would strongly suggest that they have strong male positive influences in their young men's lives. We have so many single mothers out there now and a lot of them have young boys who really have no father figures, strong male figures. We as a black people don't take up the slack with programs like Big Brothers and those kinds of programs. Those little kids just get lost out there. That is sad. So, if I could say something to them, make sure you have a husband and before you have any children, so that your children can have both parents. Of course there are a lot of young men who have been brought up without a father who have done well because the mothers have been quite capable. Somewhere in there was a grandfather, uncle, somebody, coach, somebody that significantly influenced them, set an example.

Mrs. White, mother of two sons (20, 14) and two daughters (24, 10).

Let them be their own person. Some parents want to control their kids, don't want to have nothing to do with them. Just be behind them, let them be the people they are, the person they are and just let them grow up and hope that you tried your best. It's rough being a parent, trying to raise kids. Just let them be their own people. I don't believe in controlling them that much. You have to control them to some degree but you also have to let them live. Help them through their life.

Joshua (14), son of Mrs. White.

Just take care the best you can.

Ms. Jones, mother of a son (12) and daughter (10).

They should raise their children in the home the same, whatever morals and responsibilities. They also need boy things like baseball and basketball so let him play basketball, Little League type things so he can be around his gender. That's important. To learn as much as they can about the difference of the sexes. I'm learning that now.

Mrs. Alison, mother of eight boys (20, 18, 12, 8, 6, 3, 2, 1).

I stand on the side of an adult every time. If an adult tells me that my child did this or that, I find out first.

I do my own little investigation and find out if it's true or not, then I get with the adult. 'I'm glad you came and told me. I will deal with it.' I let my kids know, no matter what, you have to respect your elders. You cannot walk around telling grown ups, teachers, any adult period anything that's disrespectful.

Mrs. Price, mother of two sons (25, 8).

Consistency, listen to them, spend some time with them, being an example around them, try to keep them around other positive African American males, African American females. Keep them always from a lot of the mess, a lot of the trash. I would tell anybody and I see young men right now, you can tell they have not been under consistency. All the time, you have to be consistent. I see that's been a problem with our young African American men. There's nobody to be consistent with. No one sets limits. Set limits.

Ms. Carr, mother of five sons (foster children, two of whom she's had since birth) ages 17, 15, 11, 10, 8.

What I suggest they do, if they don't have a nice Black male in their family, they should go to church and find a male mentor for those children. You'd be surprised how Black male mentors can influence the children and help them. And give them some kind of self-worth, give them something to look forward to because a lot of times you can have men in your household or you don't have any at all. You can do a lot as a Black woman if you want to but you can't let failure run across your mind because that's not acceptable for children. If you're a failure yourself, they will be a failure themselves so the best thing I can tell you is to take them to church, take them to some of the programs at the Imani Academy or take them to some of those places that you will find Black men doing something.

Mrs. Eve, mother of three sons (40, 34, and one died at 26) and two daughters (42, 38).

First thing I would say, and I'm sure I'm kinda guilty on that because I didn't always listen, but listen to what they have to say. They have a valid point as well as we do but I say, 'Shut up and let me talk.' That was then. As you have children, you grow, you learn, as you get older you learn. No one teaches you how to be a parent. They don't come with instructions, you learn that. What I would say to parents now, be there for them, listen to them and teach as they grow. If you don't teach them, you are their first teacher and when they get to school they already know some of the rules because the first rules and the teacher is you.

When they get to school, work with the teacher. I always did. They didn't know if I thought the teacher was wrong. I could be so mad at teachers I could break her neck or his neck but I wouldn't go along with it. I didn't let them know. That's what I would say to a single or a married mother or parent. Listen to those kids, listen to what they have to say. They have their points and if you listen and let them talk, just don't make them shut up like I did sometimes but be there for them.

Kyle (40), son of Mrs. Eve.

Be there for your kids, tell them the right thing, not only tell them but show them also. Communication is number one, a lot of these parents, I'm speaking about young parents today, they don't take time with their kids, their time is too busy for their kids. I think communication is the number one key for these kids today. I think a young parent should be there as far as communicating with their kids. Try to keep them on the right track.

Mrs. George, mother of two sons (28, 25) and two daughters (31, 30).

My advice to other mothers would be to show the children love, show them respect, discipline them, set rules and guidelines and I think if they would do those things, they would find out that their children would pretty much be successful in life.

Chapman (25), son of Mrs. George.

Be there for them, figuratively and literally. In terms of them needing you to be there in whatever type of support needed. Literally in just the amount of time you need to be there. For me it was most important that my mother was there both physically and literally. When I came home from school, she was there.

Ms. Harper, mother of a son (13).

To praise them all the time. Let them know you love them. Even though they act like they don't like it, they love it. That you are in their corner. If they do wrong or right, you're there. Be honest with them as much as you can. That's from my own experience basically, just to be honest; who I am, what I want from him. I know what kind of person you can become but you have to want it too. Let the child know that you are doing this for yourself. I want it but you are just a child, I am going to love you regardless. I will always love you. I don't want to get to the point in my life where I don't like you just because you're my sons, I don't always have to like you. You don't have to always like me but for right now we have to deal with this. The best advice I can give to another person is just let your child know that you are backing him up 100 percent. You have to go the extra mile; sometimes, you really got to go that extra mile sometimes. Award them, talk to them, let them know what you're doing. Let a child know a little about you.

Mrs. Miller, mother of a son (29).

Just first of all I would say that spiritual models are really important. That we practice what we preach, that we model goodness before our children, that we be

189

willing to say we're sorry, that we don't let them think that everything is always OK. I never let my son think that I had more than what I had. He knew what we had, we worked for him. Spend quality time with them, loving them yet disciplining them. Discipline is important because it's going to really shape them into who they'll become. I'm not talking about hitting or being abusive, I'm talking about really disciplining them. Yes, he got spankings, but I did not have to do a lot of spanking because we did a lot of talking and that's where it worked for us.

Donald (29), son of Mrs. Miller.

That's interesting, the climate in which I was raised in is very different than this one we have now. I have friends who are single dads, I have friends who have kids everywhere and I guess in all honesty the first thing I would share with a woman in that situation would be to develop some type of relationship with the Lord because ultimately whether or not you bring another male into the home or whether or not you put in the presence of another male, by one way or another, it's really going to be the Lord who ultimately orchestrates what happens. I look at friends who have kids who are single and they struggle and they have challenges, and every other week there's a new man coming in the house and some they keep men totally away and that's like they're so bruised themselves, they don't know how to really bond with a man so my thing is that it's a heavy question.

I would tell the woman to be strong but you can't be a man. All you can be is a strong woman. Put a child, especially a male child, put him in arenas that will let him see Black men who are doing something, who are men of integrity, who have standards, who have quality, who stand for and represent something that is strong and if they don't, unfortunately a lot of our women who are single parents are bruised either when they're young or the young ones still have to get the youthfulness out of them, so they don't spend quality time with their kids a lot because they are still kids. Then the older ones that are bruised, the bruised tend to pass on bruise and so it's difficult.

A lot of people don't have support systems. My mother and I had support systems, we had our whole family. It wasn't like as soon as I was born, there was me and my mama and the county. My mom worked, we lived in a house with grandparents, everybody took care of everybody. Everybody doesn't get that, everybody doesn't have that opportunity and so it's difficult and it depends on the situation that you're in with being a single parent.

I'm running into more single fathers who are single parents. That is powerful. Be brave and really fall in heavy with a relationship with the Lord because when things don't seem right and you don't know exactly what decision to make about that child, you are going to need the Lord! You're going to need Him to say, this is where I want you to take him, this is what I want you to do for her, this is how I want you to go. If not, the world offers too many different suggestions and some of them are good and some of them aren't. You could end up making some bad decisions that are very key, are very important and monumental.

I think every child has at least one thing in his life that's happened that they didn't forget. Something that shakes him and we have to be careful and guard how we handle, especially if you are a single mother. You could be a mother who just says, I don't trust men—you will pass that onto your child. He or she won't trust men. You have a potential of raising a punk. Or raising a womanizer. I have a friend whose mother raised him and she let him get away with everything. She helped lie for him, she helped cover for him and all this stuff, now all this man who is 30 years old is just a womanizer. Women everywhere. You learn that from your mom because she teaches you how to respect yourself, respect other people. She helps you disrespect other people.

Once, I tried to get on the phone, 'Mom, tell her I'm not home.' 'I'm not going to lie for you to disrespect, I'm not going to lie on that girl for you. If you want to lie, you lie on your own.' Because when it comes back, it just hits you.

There are a lot of things I would possibly say, not necessarily out of experience, more out of how just being perceptive and how people handle the situation. My mother did a hell of a job and I know that. I could easily pass on things that she did for other people. Every situation is totally different, they end up going down the same road sometimes, but every situation and every family unit is so different based on the hurt of the mother or where the mother is in her mind, her heart, her spirit, and all that stuff. You throw all that stuff together and there are some things I could possibly share but then there are a lot of things I would be totally unfamiliar to. I didn't have to go through that, a different man every week. I didn't experience that. My mother was not only guarding me from the world but she was guarding me from an emotional standpoint. She didn't want to throw me off. 'Mama, who was that? And who are you? How are you going to whup me, you don't know me!' I've seen people do that, friends and people in my life fall into that trap because of their own struggles so I would probably be a better listener to a woman who was raising a child by herself, a counselor of any kind to give advice. Where are you? That's a heavy question all on its own. That's panel discussion stuff!

Dr. Washington (51), son of Mrs. Philips.

I would advise them if at all possible to find a mentor that will work with them. Whether it's an uncle, some official in the Nation of Islam, a church, a principal, or a teacher, someone that they respect that will be willing to spend some quantity time with the child. I say quantity as opposed to quality, parents need input, it's like looking at a mirror one time and they get very frustrated and it's a very difficult job. I think it's the greatest job in the world to try to raise a child and if they could actually find someone that they could honestly, openly trust, to start giving their child advice and they also be willing to hear the advice, also say to the child, 'hey I'm sorry, I made a mistake too,' because that will occur.

The role of a parent is to provide guidance for the child, and in that we will all make some mistakes and if we see our mistakes as growth and admit those in front of the child, both the child can respect you and they will learn to apologize when they make errors. I would say that it's really not the amount of money but it's the quality of time and would be willing to spend time when the television is turned off and have a meal at the table where all members of the family sit down and talk with each other.

If it's religious faith, take the time to take the child to church, to the temple, and be willing to listen to the child. The child might not agree with them in terms of what they see and how religion is practiced today and I think that is a very key interest. Also be conscientious of the child's music and the movies. The mother should not encourage children to have movies or entertainment that would put another member of the family down. When we put the woman down, we also put the whole family down. I think that is important. I think the time that one needs just to listen to the child because throughout that many of their own problems are resolved within their own head. We have the capabilities, it's like actually trying to put ourselves in neutral and slow down a little bit. My biggest fear is that society moves us all too fast.

Ms. Evers, mother of sons (8, 8, 5).

I don't know yet, we'll see. A lot of people tell me that I must be doing a pretty good job because the boys are OK. I would just say encourage them in the things they're interested in, spend time with them as much as you can because they are only little for a while. When they're ten and you can't and you will want to. Be close with them, be firm with them. I don't know the difference between sons and daughters because I don't have girls so I can just say they are going to challenge you even when they're 15, 16, so don't let up. If you're right about it, just keep doing it and they'll drive you crazy, but just keep doing it and stick with it and don't let them wear you down.

Ms. Homes, mother of a son (10) and a daughter (9).

I am so tired of this phrase but it's true. It takes a village to raise a child. It takes a village of black positive males at the head to raise a black male child. I would say a strong support system, strong family values, start from out of the womb, from the beginning and keep building on that foundation and keep that foundation growing as far as it can go both this way and that way and this way so that child can be secure. The world is going to change. I feel a time real soon that the original man is going to get his place back. It's just through nature, it may not be in my lifetime, it may not be in my son's lifetime but it will be in the lifetime of my family. I want it to be passed on.

Tyri (10), son of Ms. Homes.

Always love them and when they ask for a hug then you should give it to them because they are probably sad or something.

Mrs. Little, mother of two biological sons (40, 37), an adopted son she has raised since he was four (now 15), and a daughter (32).

I think I would give them some of the basics I used. The only thing I would change is there must be a home with peace and harmony between the parents. If not then the mother can do it on her own. You put God first, you put your trust in Him, you stress education, you stress respect from your children. I do believe if a child is wrong, he needs to be spanked. I still believe in the old fashioned way of raising children. This is what I would tell them.

REFERENCES

Akbar, N. (1982). Miseducation to education. Jersey City, NJ: New Mind Productions.

Akbar, N. (1984). Chains and images of psychological slavery. Jersey City, NJ: Mind Productions & Associates, Inc.

Akbar, N. (1991). Visions for Black men. Tallahassee, FL: Mind Productions & Associates, Inc.

Akbar, N. (1994). Light from ancient Africa. Tallahassee, FL: Mind Productions & Associates, Inc.

Allen, W. (1985). Race, income and family dynamics: A study of adolescent male socialization processes and outcomes. In M. Spencer, G. Brookins, & W. Allen (Eds.), Beginnings: The social and affective development of Black children. Hillsdale, NJ: Lawrence Erlbaum Associates, Publishers.

American Psychological Association. (1994). Publication Manual of the American Psychological Association (4th ed.). Washington, DC: American Psychological Association.

Baker-Fletcher, G. (1996). Xodus: African American male journey. Minneapolis: Fortress Press.

Bandura, A. (1986). Social foundations of thought and action: A social cognitive theory. Englewood Cliffs, NJ: Prentice-Hall.

Bem, S. (1984). Androgyny and gender theory: A conceptual and empirical interrogation. Nebraska Symposium on Motivation.

Bem, S. (1987). Yes: Probing the promise of androgyny. In M. Walsh (Ed.), The psychology of women: Ongoing debates. New Haven, CT: Yale university Press

ben-Jochannan, J. (1981). Black Man of the Nile. New York: Alkebu-lan Books.

Berry, G. & Asamen, J. (Eds.). (1993). Children & Television: Images in a changing sociocultural world. Newbury Park: Sage Publications.

Billingsley, A. (1992). Climbing Jacob's ladder: The enduring legacy of African-American families. New York: Simon & Schuster.

Boyd-Franklin, N. (1989) Black families in therapy: A multisystems approach. New York: Guilford.

Breitman, G. (1965). Malcolm X speaks. New York: Grove Press, INC.

Broverman, K., Vogel, S., Broverman, D., Clarkson, R., & Rosenkrantz, P. (1972). Sex role stereotypes: A current appraisal. Journal of Social Issues, 28.

Browder, A. (1989). From the Browder File: 22 essays on the African American experience. Washington, DC: The Institute of Karmic Guidance.

Burgess, N. (1995). Female-headed households in sociol-historical perspective. In B. Dickerson (Ed.), African American single mothers: Understanding their lives and families. Thousand Oaks: Sage Publications.

Bush, L. (1995). Africentric Independent Black Institutions: A means to social justice? In A. Darder (Ed.), Bicultural Studies in Education: Transgressive discourses of resistance and possibility. Claremont, CA.: The Institute for Education in Transformation.

Bush, L. (1997). Independent Black institutions in America: A rejection of schooling, an opportunity for education. Urban Education, 32.

Cannon, K. (1988). Black Womanist Ethics. Atlanta: Scholars Press.

Carruthers, J. (1994). Black Intellectuals and the Crisis in Black Education. In M. Shujaa (Ed), Too much Schooling too little Education: A paradox of Black life in white societies. Trenton, NJ: African World Press, Inc.

Carson, B. (1990). Gifted hands. New York: Harper Paperbacks.

Clark, R. (1983). Family Life and School Achievement: Why poor Black children succeed or fail. Chicago: The University of Chicago Press.

Chavez, D. (1986). Perpetuation of gender inequality: A content analysis of comic strips.

Collins, P. (1994). The meaning of motherhood in Black culture. In R. Staples (Ed.), The Black family: Essays and studies (5th ed.) (pp. 165-173). Belmont, CA: Wadsworth Publishing Company, Inc.

Collins, P. (1990). Black Feminist Thought: Knowledge, consciousness, and the politics of empowerment (vol. 2) Boston: Unwin Hyman.

Comstock, G., & Paik, H. (1991). Television and the American child. New York: Academic Press.
Darder, A. (1991). Culture and Power in the Classroom. Westport, Connecticut: Bergin & Garvey.
Davidson, N. (1990). Life without a father: America's greatest social catastrophe. Policy Review, 5.
Dickerson, B. (1995). African American single mothers: Understanding their lives and families. Thousand Oaks: Sage Publications.
Dines, G., & Humez, J. (Ed.). (1995). Gender, Race and Class in Media: A text-reader. Thousand Oaks: Sage Publications.
Diop, C. (1974). African Origin of Civilization: Myth or reality. New York: Lawrence Hill.
Dorr, A. (1983). No Shortcuts to Judging Reality. In P.E. Bryant & S. Anderson (Eds.), Watching and understanding TV: Research on children's attention and comprehension. New York: Academic Press.
Douglass, F. (1988). Narrative of the Life of Frederick Douglass: An American slave. Cambridge, Massachusetts: The Belknap Press of Harvard University Press.
Doyle, J. (1989). The Male Experience (2nd edition). Dubuque, IA: W.C. Brown.
Du Bois, W.E.B. (1898). The Study of the Negro problem. Annals, AAPSS, 1, 1-23.
Du Bois, W.E.B. (1909). The Negro American Family (Reprinted 1970). Cambridge, MA: The MIT press.
Duncan, G. (1994). The Light Before the Dawn. Unpublished doctoral dissertation, The Claremont Graduate School.
Ellison, R. (1952). Invisible man. New York: The New American Library, Inc.
Essence Magazine. (1997, November). Do our children need fathers? Copy Editor.
Flavell, J., Green, F., & Flavell, E. (1990). Developmental changes in young children's knowledge about the mind. Cognitive Development.
Forcey, L. (1987). Mothers of Sons: Toward an understanding of responsibility. New York: Praeger.
Franklin, C. (1984). The Changing Definition of Masculinity. New York: Plenum.
Franklin, C. (1988). Men and Society. Chicago: Nelson Hall.

Franklin, C. (1994). Men's studies, the men's movement, and the study of Black masculinities: Further demystification of masculinities in America. In. R. Majors. & J. Gordon. (Eds.), The American Black male: His present status and future. Chicago: Nelson-Hall Publishers.

Frazier, F. (1966). The Negro family in the United States. Chicago University of Chicago Press.

Freimuth, M., & Horenstein, G. (1982). A critical examination of the concept of gender.

Freud, S. (1972). Three Essays on the Theory of Sexuality (J. Strachey, Ed.). New York: Avon Books. (Original work published in 1905)

Gary, L. (1981). Black Men. Beverly Hills: Sage Publications.

George, S. & Dickerson, B. (1995). The role of the grandmother in poor single-mother families and households. In B. Dickerson (Ed.), African American Single Mothers: Understanding their lives and families. (pp. 146-163) Thousand Oaks: Sage Publications.

Gibbs, J. (1984). Black Adolescents and Youth: An endangered species. American Journal of Orthopsychiatry.

Giroux, H. (1988). Schooling and the Struggle for Public Life: Critical pedagogy in the modern age. Minneapolis: University of Minnesota Press.

Graves, S. (1993). Television, the portrayal of African Americans, and the development of children's attitudes. In G. Berry & J. Asamen (Eds.), Children & Television: Images in a changing sociocultural world. Newbury Park: Sage Publications.

Grier, W., & Cobbs, P. (1968). Black Rage. New York: Basic Books, Inc., Publishers.

Gutman, H. (1976). The Black family in Slavery and Freedom: 1750-1925. New York: Pantheon.

Hall, S. (1995). The White of Their Eyes: Racist ideologies in the media. In G. Dines & J. Humez (Eds.), Gender, race and class in the media: A text reader. Thousand

Oaks, CA: Sage Publications.

Hare, N. (1971). The frustrated masculinity of Negro male. In R. Staples (Ed.), The Black family. Belmont, California: Wadsworth Publishing Company.

Harris, M. (1992). Africentrism and Curriculum: Concepts, issues, and prospects. Journal of Negro Education, 62, 301-316.

Henderson, B. (1990, May 21). A Radical Proposal for Black boys: separate classes. Time.

Hetherington, M. (1991). Coping with family transitions: Winners, losers, and survivors. In S. Chess, & M. Hertzig (Eds.), Annual progress in child psychiatry and child development. New York: Brunner/Mazel Publishers

Hill, P. (1992). Coming of Age: An African American rites-of-passage. Chicago: African American Images.

Hill, R. (1993). Research on the African American family: Holistic perspective. Westport, Connecticut: Auburn House.

Hill, R. (1997). The Strength of African American families: Twenty-five years later. Washington, D.C.: R & B Publishing.

Hill, R. (ed.). (1987). The Marcus Garvey and Universal Negro Improvement Association. Berkeley, Los Angeles, London: University of California Press.

Holland, S. (1991). Positive Role Models for Primary-Grade Black inner-city males. Equity and Excellence.

hooks, b. (1981). Ain't I a Woman: Black women and feminism. Boston: South End Press.

hooks, b. (1990). Yearning: Race, gender, and cultural politics. Boston: South End Press.

hooks, b. (1994). Teaching to Transgress: Education as the practice of freedom. New York: Routledge.

Hunter, A., & Davis, J. (1992). Constructing gender: An exploration of Afro-American men's conceptualization of manhood. Gender and Society.

Hunter, A., & Davis, J. (1994). Hidden voices of Black

men: The meaning, structure and complexity of manhood. Journal of Black Studies.

Hurlock, E. (1964). Child Development. (4th ed.) New York: McGraw-Hill.

Hutchinson, E. (1994). The Assassination of the Black Male Image. Los Angeles, CA: Middle Passage Press.

Hyde, B. & Texidor, M. (1994). A Description of the Fathering Experience among Black fathers. In R. Staples (Ed.), The Black family: Essays and studies (5th ed.).

Jackson, J. (1970). Introduction to African civilizations. New Jersey: Citadel Press.

Jones, D. (1992). The Black holocaust. Philadelphia: Hikeka Press, Inc.

June, L. (Ed.). (1991). The Black family: Past, present, and future. Grand Rapids, Michigan: Zondervan Publishing House.

Karenga, M. (1980). Kawaida Theory: An introductory outline. Inglewood, CA: Kawaida Publications.

Katz, J. (1995). Advertisement and the construction of violent white masculinity. In G. Dines & J. Humez (Eds.), Gender, race and class in the media: A text reader. Thousand Oaks, CA: Sage Publications.

King, J. & Mitchell, C. (1990) Black Mothers to Sons: Juxtaposing African-American literature with social practice. New York: Peter Lang.

King, J. & Mitchell, C. (1991) Black mothers to Sons: Juxtaposing African-American literature with social practice. In Bowser (Ed.), Black male adolescence: Parenting and education in community context. New York: University Press of America.

Kohlberg, K. (1966). Cognitive-development analysis of children's sex-role concepts attitudes. In E. E. Maccoby (Ed.) The development of sex differences. Stanford, California: Stanford University Press.

Kunjufu, J. (1994). Countering the Conspiracy to Destroy Black Boys (Series). Chicago: African American Images.

202

Kunjufu, J. (1995). Adam! Where are you. Chicago: African American Images.

Lapsley, D. (1990). Continuity and discontinuity in adolescent social cognitive development. In R. Montemayor, G. Adams, & T. Gullotta (Eds.), Advances in adolescent development: Vol. 2 From childhood to adolescence: A transitional period? Newbury Park: Sage.

Lee, C. (1987). Black Manhood Training: Group counseling for Black Males grades 7-12. Journal for Specialists in Group Work, 12.

Lewis, M., & Weinraub, M. (1979). Origin of Early Sex-Role Development. Sex Roles, 5.

Liebow, E. (1967). Tally's Corner. Boston: Little Brown.

Lindsay, L. (1978). Methodology and Change: Problems of applied social science research techniques in the Commonwealth Caribbean. Mona, Jamaica: University of the West Indies.

Madhubuti, H. (1990). Black Men: Obsolete, Single, Dangerous. Chicago. Third World Press.

Malveaux, J. (1988). The economic status of Black families. In H. McAdoo (Ed.), Black Families (2nd ed.). Newbury Park: Sage Publications.

Mamay, P. D., & Simpson, R. L. (1981). Three Female Roles in Television Commercials. Sex Roles, 7.

Marable, M. (1994). The Black male: Searching beyond stereotypes. In R. Majors & J. Gordon. (Eds.), The American Black Male: His present status and future. Chicago: Nelson-Hall Publishers.

Mauer, M. (1994). A generation behind bars: Black males and the criminal justice system. In R. Majors & J. Gordon. (Eds.), The American Black male: His present status and future (pp.81-94). Chicago: Nelson-Hall Publishers.

McAdoo, H. (1981). Black father and child interactions. In L. Gary (Ed.). Black men. Beverly Hills, CA: Sage Publications.

McAdoo, H. (1988). Black Families (2nd ed.). Newbury Park: Sage Publications.

McLoyd, V., Jayaratne, T., Ceballo, R., & Borquez, J. (1994). Unemployment and work interruption among African American single mothers: Effects on parenting and adolescent socio-emotional functioning. Child Development.

McLoyd, V. & Wilson, L. (1990). Maternal behavior, social support, and economic conditions as predictors of distress in children. New Directions for Child Development.

McGhee, P., & Frueh, T. (1980). Television viewing and the learning of Sex-Role Stereotypes. Sex Roles.

McKenna, M., Kear, D., & Ellsworth, R. (1991). Developmental trends in children's use of print media: a national study. National Reading Conference Yearbook, 40.

Meltzoff, A. (1988). Imitation of television models by infants. Child Development.

Midgette, T. (1993). African-American male academies: A positive view. Journal of Multicultural Counseling and Development.

Minuchin, S. (1974). Families and family therapy. Cambridge, MA: Harvard University Press.

Money, J. (1995). Gendermaps: Social constructionism, feminism, and sexosophical history. New York: Continuum.

Moynihan, D. P. (1965). The Negro Family: The case for national action. U.S. Department of Labor: Office of Planning and Research.

Muhammad, E. (1965). Message to the Blackman in America. Newport News, Virginia: United Brothers Communications Systems.

Nobles, W. (1980). African Philosophy: Foundations for the Black psychology. In R. Jones (Ed.), Black Psychology. New York: Harper & Row.

Nobles, W. (1988). African American Family Life: An instrument of culture. In H. McAdoo (Ed.), Black Families. Beverly Hills, CA: Sage.

Nobles, W., Goddard, L., Cavil, W., & George, P. (1987). African-American families: Issues, insights and directions. Oakland, CA: Black Family Institute.

Ogbu, J. (1991). Immigrant and involuntary minorities in comparative perspective. In M. Gibson &, J. Ogbu, (Eds). Minority status and schooling: A comparative study of immigrant and involuntary minorities. New York: Garland Publishing, Inc.

Oliver, W. (1984). Black males and the tough guy image: A dysfunctional compensatory adaptation. The Western Journal of Black Studies.

Parish, T. & Taylor, J. (1979). The impact of divorce and subsequent father absence on children's and adolescent's self concept's. Journal of Youth and Adolescence.

Perry, I., (1993). I am still thirsty: A theorization on the authority and cultural location of Afrocentrism. In T. Perry & J. Fraser (Eds.), Freedom's Plow. New York: Routledge.

Perry, D. G. & Bussey, K. (1984). Social Development. Englewood Cliffs, NJ: Prentice-Hall.

Pettigrew, T. (1964). A Profile of the Negro American. Princeton, NJ: Van Nostrand.

Pleck, J. (1976). The male sex role: Definition, problems and sources of change. Journal of Social Issues.

Pleck, J. (1981). The myth of masculinity. Cambridge: MIT Press.

Poussaint, A. (1982, August). What every Black woman should know about a Black man. Ebony.

Randolph, S. (1995). African American children in single-mother families. In B. Dickerson (Ed.), African American single mothers: Understanding their lives and families. Thousand Oaks: Sage Publications.

Roberts, G. (1994). Brother to brother: African American modes of relating among men. Journal of Black Studies.

Rochlin, G. (1980). The Masculine Dilemma. Boston: Little, Brown, and Company.

Rubin, J., Provenzano, F., & Luria, Z. (1974). The Eye of the Beholder: Parents' views on sex of newborns. American Journal of Orthopsychiatry.

Rutter, M. (1987). Psychosocial resilience and protective mechanisms. American Journal of Orthopsychiatry.

Ryan, M. (1997, May 11). If you can't teach me, don't criticize me. Parade Magazine.

Sampson, R. (1987). Urban black violence: The effect of male joblessness and family disruption. American Journal of Sociology.

Schoenberg, M. (1993). Growing up male: The psychology of masculinity. Westport, Connecticut: Bergin and Garvey.

Shujaa, J. M. (1992). Afrocentric transformation and parental choice in African American independent schools. Journal of Negro Education.

Shujaa, J. M. (1994). Too Much Schooling too Little Education: A paradox of Black life in White societies. Trenton, NJ: Africa World Press.

Sigel, E. (Ed.) (1986). Parental belief systems. Hillsdale, NJ: Erlbaum.

Snyder, J., & Patterson, G. (1986). The effects of consequences on patterns of social interaction: A quasi-experimental approach to reinforcement in natural interaction. Child Development.

Sparks, E. (1996). Overcoming stereotypes of mothers in the American context. In K. Wyche & F. Crosby, (Eds.). Women's ethnicities: Journeys through psychology. Boulder, Colorado: Westview Press.

Staples, R. (1973). The Black Woman in America. Chicago: Nelson Hill.

Staples, R. (1978a). Masculinity and race: The dual dilemma of men. Journal of Social Issues.

Staples, R. (1978b). The Myth of the Impotent Black Male. R. Staples, (Ed.). The Black family. Belmont, CA: Wadsworth Publishing Company, Inc.

Steinberg, L. (1987). Single parents, stepparents, and the susceptibility of adolescents to antisocial peer pressure. Child Development.

Stearns, R. (1990). Be a man: Males in Modern Society (2nd ed.). New York: Homes and Meier.

Stolberg, S. (1997, September 12). U.S. life expectancy hits new high. New York Times.

Stroman, C. (1991) Television's role in the socialization of African Americans and adolescence. Journal of Negro Education.

Sudarkasa, N. (1980). African and Afro-American family structure: A comparison. Black Scholar.

Sudarkasa, N. (1988). Interpreting the African heritage in Afro-American family organization. In H. McAdoo (Ed.), Black Families (2nd ed.) Newbury Park: Sage Publications.

Sudarkasa, N. (1993). Female-headed households: Some neglectful dimensions. In H. McAdoo (Ed.), Families Ethnicity: Strength in diversity. Newbury Park: Sage Publications, Inc. U.S. Bureau of the Census. (1991). Marital status and living arrangements: March 1990 (Current Population Reports, Series P-20, No. 405). Washington, DC: U.S. Government Printing Office.

Van Sertima, I. (1976). They Came before Columbus. New York: Random House.

Varma, M. (1980). Sex stereotyping in Black Play of Preschool Children. Indian Educational Review.

Wallace, M. (1991). Black Macho and the Myth of the Superwoman. New York: Verso Press.

Watson, J. (1969). Operate conditioning of visual fixation in infants under visual and auditory reinforcement. Developmental Psychology, 1.

Watts, R. (1993). Community action through manhood development: A look at concepts and concerns from the front line. American Journal of Community Psychology.

Wieder, A. (1992). Afrocentrisms: Capitalist, democratic, and liberationist. Educational Foundations.

Weiler, K. (1988). Women teaching for change: Gender, class, and power. New York: Bergin & Garvey Publishers.

Williams, C. (1987). The Destruction of Black Civilization. Chicago: Third World Press.

Wilson, A. (1978). The Developmental Psychology of the Black Child. New York: Africana Research Publications.

Wilson, M. (Ed.). (1995). African American Family Life: Its structural and ecological aspects. San Francisco: Jossey-Bass Publishers.

Woodson, C. (1977). The Mis-Education of the Negro. New York: AMS Press.

Wright, W. (1991). The Black Male Child: A threatened resource. Are all-Black male classes the answer to one of urban school's most pressing problems? Principal.

Young, I. M. (1990). Justice and Politics and Difference. New Jersey: Princeton University Press.

Zimilies, H. & Lee, V. (1991). Adolescent family structure and educational progress. Developmental Psychology.

Zimmerman, M., Salem, D., & Maton, K. (1995). Family structure and psychosocial correlates among urban African-American adolescent males. Child Development.